Canadian Living
Make It Chocolate!

EXCLUSIVE DISTRIBUTOR FOR CANADA & USA
Simon & Schuster Canada
166 King Street East, Suite 300
Toronto ON M5A 1J3
Tel: 647-427-8882
Toll Free: 800-387-0446   **simonandschuster.ca**
Fax: 647-430-9446   **canadianliving.com/books**

Cataloguing data available from
Bibliothèque et Archives nationales du Québec.

Art director: Colin Elliott
Project editor: Tina Anson Mine

02-16

Legal deposit: 2016
Bibliothèque et Archives nationales du Québec
Library and Archives Canada

ISBN 978-1-988002-25-5

Printed in Canada

Government of Quebec – Tax credit for book publishing –
Administered by SODEC.
sodec.gouv.qc.ca

This publisher gratefully acknowledges the support of the
Société de développement des enterprises culturelles du Québec.

Canada Council   Conseil des arts
for the Arts   du Canada

We gratefully acknowledge the support of the
Canada Council for the Arts for its publishing program.

We acknowledge the financial support of our publishing activities
by the Government of Canada through the Canada Book Fund.

Canadian Living
Make It Chocolate!

BY THE CANADIAN LIVING TEST KITCHEN

JUNIPER
PUBLISHING
A Quebecor Media Corporation

From Our Test Kitchen

There is no ingredient quite like chocolate. It is simultaneously sexy and comforting, finicky and forgiving, rustic and sophisticated.

Like the little black dress of the culinary world, chocolate can be dressed up or down for any occasion. It can be the luscious base for an elegant dessert at a fancy dinner party or the starting point for a simple hot chocolate to sip with your family in your pajamas. No matter what you crave—something gooey, creamy, crunchy, chewy, melty, buttery, chilly or cakey—chocolate can deliver.

Canadian Living has—literally—thousands of Tested-Till-Perfect chocolate recipes. We reviewed every luxurious one to create this essential collection. It was such a delicious experience putting together this all-time favourite book. We wish you the ooiest, gooiest of culinary adventures as you find your favourites among our favourites.

Eat well and enjoy!

Annabelle

ANNABELLE WAUGH
FOOD DIRECTOR

THE CANADIAN LIVING TEST KITCHEN

AMANDA BARNIER **JENNIFER BARTOLI** **IRENE FONG** **GILEAN WATTS**

Chocolate
Bar Brownies
page 65

"There is no ingredient quite like chocolate. It is simultaneously sexy and comforting, finicky and forgiving, rustic and sophisticated."

We've grouped our best chocolate recipes by the predominant texture you experience when you take a bite. To search by type of treat, such as brownies or cookies, turn to the index on page 153.

Contents

Choosing & Using Chocolate

BUY THE BEST CHOCOLATE YOU CAN AFFORD

We use high-quality chocolate in all of our recipes. It costs more to buy premium brands, such as Lindt or Callebaut, but they taste better and are easier to work with. They contain real cocoa butter (not vegetable fat), which melts more smoothly and results in glossier glazes, candies and more.

GRATING & SHAVING CHOCOLATE

For a finely textured chocolate garnish, grate chocolate on the fine side of a box grater. To make delicate shreds with a coarser texture, shave the edge of a chocolate bar with a vegetable peeler. The heat of your hands will melt grated or shaved chocolate; to avoid this, grate or shave it over a piece of waxed paper and use a spoon to sprinkle the pieces over your desserts.

USE THE RIGHT KNIFE

When you're chopping chocolate for melting, use a sharp, heavy chef's knife. Chop the chocolate into pieces the size of almonds or smaller. The tinier the pieces, the more quickly and smoothly they will melt.

CHOCOLATE VARIETIES

All types of chocolate contain one or more of the following building blocks: **cocoa liquor, cocoa butter, milk and sugar.** Here's the info you need to know about the different varieties of chocolate.

UNSWEETENED

Also called baking chocolate, this is pure, unsweetened chocolate liquor cooled and moulded into blocks. It is bitter and cannot be used interchangeably with semisweet or bittersweet chocolate.

BITTERSWEET & SEMISWEET

These chocolates contain pure chocolate liquor, cocoa butter, sugar, vanilla and lecithin (a stabilizer). In baking, both types are interchangeable, although bittersweet has a more pronounced chocolate flavour.

DARK

This is a catch-all term for chocolate that contains a high amount of cocoa liquor. It comes in a number of varieties, which are described on the label in terms of cocoa percentage. Our recipes often call for dark chocolate with 70% cocoa because it has a beautiful balance between bitterness, sweetness and rich flavour.

MORE: FOR TIPS ON TEMPERING CHOCOLATE, SEE PAGE 82.

MELTING CHOCOLATE

With its high cocoa butter content, chocolate must be handled gently when melting so it doesn't curdle, scorch or lose its shine. Here is how to melt any type of chocolate successfully.

Chop finely » Pieces the size of almonds or a bit smaller melt quickly. Place them in a heatproof glass or stainless-steel bowl with a rim just slightly larger than the rim of the saucepan that will be underneath it. (If the bowl is too large, the burner may heat it and burn the chocolate.)

Simmer gently » Pour enough water into the pan to come 1 inch (2.5 cm) up the side. Make sure the bottom of the bowl doesn't touch the water in the pan. Place the pan over medium heat; heat the water just until it's steaming (not boiling). Place the bowl over the pan. Let it stand just until three-quarters of the chocolate is melted.

Stir well » Remove the bowl from the saucepan and stir until the remaining chocolate is melted.

Do not cover » Moisture droplets can accumulate on the lid and drop into the chocolate, causing it to seize (see What Is Seizing?, right).

What Is Seizing?

Moisture and high heat are chocolate's mortal enemies. If any liquid gets into the chocolate, or it's cooked over too-high heat, chocolate will clump, or seize, into an unusable mass. To prevent this, make sure all of your bowls and utensils are perfectly dry and that your heatproof bowl completely covers the lip of the saucepan so that steam doesn't touch the mixture. Keeping the water hot but not boiling reduces steam and helps to ensure success.

WHITE

This type contains cocoa butter but no chocolate liquor. The cocoa butter is what makes good-quality white chocolate ivory or cream coloured. Less-expensive brands are often whiter because vegetable fats have replaced some or all of the cocoa butter. Check the ingredient list when buying white chocolate; a good bar will contain cocoa butter, sugar, dry milk solids and vanilla.

SWEET

This type of chocolate contains the same ingredients as semisweet chocolate, but has a higher sugar content.

SIFTING COCOA POWDER

Some containers of cocoa powder are lumpier than others. Sifting cocoa before adding it to other ingredients removes the lumps and ensures that it will seamlessly incorporate into the recipe. It's a step you can do anytime you're baking, whether the recipe calls for it specifically or not.

MILK

This chocolate contains the same ingredients as semisweet, bittersweet and sweet chocolate, plus dry or concentrated milk. It is popular for eating out of hand.

COCOA POWDER

Made of ground, partially defatted cocoa solids, cocoa powder comes in two types: natural (usually labelled unsweetened cocoa powder) and Dutch-processed, which has been treated to neutralize its natural acidity. Cocoa powder should not be replaced with hot chocolate powders or mixes.

Chocolate Cheesecake With Caramel Pecan Sauce

HANDS-ON TIME	TOTAL TIME	MAKES
45 MINUTES	7 HOURS	16 SERVINGS

What you need

1 cup	graham cracker crumbs
⅓ cup	finely chopped pecans
¼ cup	butter, melted

CHEESECAKE:

¾ cup	packed brown sugar
3	pkg (each 250 g) cream cheese, softened
4	eggs
1 tsp	vanilla
2	bars (each 100 g) 70% dark chocolate, melted
¼ cup	whipping cream (35%)

CARAMEL PECAN SAUCE:

¾ cup	granulated sugar
½ cup	whipping cream (35%)
2 tbsp	butter
⅓ cup	pecan halves, toasted and halved
pinch	salt

NUTRITIONAL INFORMATION, PER SERVING: about 451 cal, 7 g pro, 34 g total fat (19 g sat. fat), 33 g carb, 2 g fibre, 124 mg chol, 224 mg sodium, 145 mg potassium. % RDI: 7% calcium, 22% iron, 27% vit A, 8% folate.

How to make it

Grease then line side of 9-inch (2.5 L) springform pan with parchment paper. Centre pan on large square of heavy-duty foil; bring foil up and press to side of pan.

Stir together graham cracker crumbs, pecans and butter until moistened; press onto bottom of prepared pan. Bake in 350°F (180°C) oven until firm, about 10 minutes. Let cool in pan on rack.

CHEESECAKE: Press brown sugar through sieve to remove any lumps. In bowl, beat cream cheese with brown sugar on high for 5 minutes, scraping down side of bowl often. Beat in eggs, 1 at a time. Beat in vanilla.

Mix about 1 cup of the cream cheese mixture into chocolate until smooth; return to remaining cheese mixture and stir until combined. Beat in cream. Pour over crust.

Set pan in larger pan; pour in enough hot water to come 1 inch (2.5 cm) up side. Bake in 325°F (160°C) oven until set around edge and centre is still jiggly, about 1 hour.

Transfer springform pan to rack and remove foil; let cool completely. Cover and refrigerate until firm and chilled, about 4 hours. (Make-ahead: Refrigerate for up to 24 hours.)

CARAMEL PECAN SAUCE: In heavy saucepan, stir sugar with ¼ cup water over medium heat until dissolved. Bring to boil; boil vigorously, without stirring but brushing down side of pan often with pastry brush dipped in cold water, until dark amber, 6 to 10 minutes. Remove from heat.

Standing back and averting face, add cream; whisk until smooth. Whisk in butter until smooth. Stir in pecans and salt. Let cool. (Make-ahead: Refrigerate in airtight container for up to 24 hours; gently rewarm to liquefy.)

Serve sauce over cheesecake.

Maple Chocolate Butter Tarts

HANDS-ON TIME	TOTAL TIME	MAKES
25 MINUTES	2 HOURS	12 TARTS

What you need

¾ cup	packed brown sugar
½ cup	maple syrup (No. 1 medium grade)
⅓ cup	butter, melted
2	eggs
1 tbsp	cider vinegar
½ tsp	salt
½ cup	chopped walnut halves
½ cup	chopped bittersweet chocolate or semisweet chocolate chips

SOUR CREAM PASTRY:

1¼ cups	all-purpose flour
¼ tsp	salt
¼ cup	cold butter, cubed
¼ cup	cold lard, cubed
2 tbsp	ice water (approx)
4 tsp	sour cream

How to make it

SOUR CREAM PASTRY: In bowl, whisk flour with salt. Using pastry blender, cut in butter and lard until in fine crumbs with a few larger pieces. Whisk ice water with sour cream; drizzle over flour mixture, tossing briskly with fork and adding more water if necessary to form ragged dough. Press into disc; wrap and refrigerate until chilled, about 30 minutes. (*Make-ahead: Refrigerate for up to 3 days.*)

On lightly floured surface, roll out pastry to generous ⅛-inch (3 mm) thickness. Using 4-inch (10 cm) round cutter, cut out 12 circles, rerolling and cutting scraps. Fit circles into 12 muffin cups; refrigerate for 30 minutes.

Meanwhile, whisk together brown sugar, maple syrup, butter, eggs, vinegar and salt. Divide walnuts and chocolate among pastry shells. Spoon scant ¼ cup filling into each shell.

Bake in 350°F (180°C) oven until filling is set and pastry is golden, 20 to 25 minutes. Run thin knife around edges to release tarts. Let cool in pan on rack for 20 minutes. Transfer to rack; let cool completely. (*Make-ahead: Store in single layer in airtight container for up to 24 hours.*)

NUTRITIONAL INFORMATION, PER TART: about 343 cal, 4 g pro, 21 g total fat (10 g sat. fat), 36 g carb, 1 g fibre, 59 mg chol, 225 mg sodium, 140 mg potassium. % RDI: 4% calcium, 11% iron, 10% vit A, 13% folate.

Slow Cooker Hot Cocoa Cake

HANDS-ON TIME	TOTAL TIME	MAKES
30 MINUTES	2¾ HOURS	12 TO 16 SERVINGS

What you need

2 cups	all-purpose flour
¾ cup	cocoa powder, sifted
1½ tsp	baking powder
1½ tsp	baking soda
½ tsp	salt
pinch	cinnamon
2 cups	granulated sugar
2	eggs
½ cup	vegetable oil
½ cup	milk
½ cup	cooled brewed coffee or water
2 tsp	vanilla
½ cup	semisweet chocolate chips

WHIPPED CREAM:

⅔ cup	whipping cream (35%)
2 tbsp	granulated sugar
½ tsp	vanilla
pinch	cinnamon

How to make it

Grease bottom of 5- to 6-quart (5 to 6 L) slow cooker; set aside.

In large bowl, whisk together flour, cocoa powder, baking powder, baking soda, salt and cinnamon. Whisk together sugar, eggs, oil, milk, coffee and vanilla until well combined. Add to flour mixture; stir just until moistened.

Pour into prepared slow cooker; sprinkle with chocolate chips. Cover and cook on high until cake tester inserted in centre comes out with a few moist crumbs clinging, about 2 hours.

Turn off slow cooker; uncover and let cool for 15 minutes.

WHIPPED CREAM: Meanwhile, whip together cream, sugar, vanilla and cinnamon until soft peaks form.

Spoon warm cake into mugs; top with whipped cream.

TIP FROM THE TEST KITCHEN
Make sure you use the slow cooker size specified in this recipe. If you use a smaller slow cooker, the cake will be too tall, and the centre won't cook through.

NUTRITIONAL INFORMATION, PER EACH OF 16 SERVINGS:
about 300 cal, 4 g pro, 13 g total fat (4 g sat. fat), 45 g carb, 2 g fibre, 37 mg chol, 234 mg sodium, 170 mg potassium. % RDI: 4% calcium, 11% iron, 5% vit A, 17% folate.

Chocolate, Caramel and Cashew Torte

HANDS-ON TIME	TOTAL TIME	MAKES
40 MINUTES	8¾ HOURS	10 TO 12 SERVINGS

What you need

½ cup	butter, softened
⅓ cup	granulated sugar
1	egg yolk
½ tsp	vanilla
¾ cup	all-purpose flour
⅓ cup	cocoa powder
¼ cup	ground roasted cashews (about ½ cup whole)
¼ tsp	baking powder
pinch	salt

CARAMEL CASHEW FILLING:

⅔ cup	granulated sugar
½ cup	whipping cream (35%)
¾ cup	chopped roasted cashews

GANACHE:

170 g	bittersweet chocolate, finely chopped
¼ cup	cold butter, cubed
¼ cup	whipping cream (35%)

How to make it

In bowl, beat butter with sugar until fluffy; beat in egg yolk and vanilla. Whisk together flour, cocoa powder, ground cashews, baking powder and salt; stir into butter mixture. Press onto bottom and up side of greased 9-inch (23 cm) round tart pan with removable bottom; refrigerate until firm, about 30 minutes.

Bake on baking sheet in 350°F (180°C) oven until surface looks dry, 30 minutes. Let cool in pan on rack. (*Make-ahead: Cover and store in cool, dry place for up to 24 hours.*)

CARAMEL CASHEW FILLING: Meanwhile, in heavy saucepan, stir sugar with 2 tbsp water over medium heat until dissolved; brush down side of pan with pastry brush dipped in cold water. Bring to boil; boil vigorously, without stirring but brushing down side of pan often, until dark amber, about 10 minutes.

Standing back and averting face, add cream; whisk until smooth. Stir in cashews; boil for 1 minute. Pour into heatproof bowl; let cool for 30 minutes. Spread over tart shell; refrigerate until set, about 2 hours.

GANACHE: Place chocolate and butter in heatproof bowl. In saucepan, bring cream just to boil over medium-high heat; pour over chocolate mixture, whisking until melted and smooth. Refrigerate until cool, 30 minutes. Pour over tart; spread evenly. Refrigerate until set, about 4 hours. (*Make-ahead: Cover and refrigerate for up to 3 days.*)

TIP FROM THE TEST KITCHEN
Adding cool cream to hot caramel causes spattering. Wear oven mitts, use a long-handled spoon and keep your face a safe distance away from the pan.

NUTRITIONAL INFORMATION, PER EACH OF 12 SERVINGS: about 414 cal, 5 g pro, 29 g total fat (15 g sat. fat), 36 g carb, 3 g fibre, 67 mg chol, 98 mg sodium, 251 mg potassium. % RDI: 3% calcium, 18% iron, 15% vit A, 10% folate.

Flourless Chocolate Lava Cakes

HANDS-ON TIME	TOTAL TIME	MAKES
30 MINUTES	3 HOURS	12 SERVINGS

What you need

340 g	bittersweet chocolate or semisweet chocolate, chopped
½ cup	butter, cubed
	seeds of 1 vanilla pod
2 cups	granulated sugar
6	eggs
6	egg yolks
¼ cup	cocoa powder, sifted
pinch	salt
340 g	strawberries, hulled and diced
	whipped cream (optional)

How to make it

In heatproof bowl over hot (not boiling) water, melt chocolate with butter, stirring until smooth. Stir in vanilla seeds. Remove from heat.

Whisk in sugar. Whisk in eggs and egg yolks, 1 at a time. Whisk in cocoa powder and salt. Pour into twelve ¾-cup (175 mL) ramekins; place on rimmed baking sheet. (*Make-ahead: Cover and refrigerate for up to 24 hours. Bake as directed, adding 5 minutes to baking time.*)

Bake in 425°F (220°C) oven until edges are set and centres are slightly jiggly when lightly tapped, about 15 minutes. Let cool on pan on rack for 3 minutes.

Run knife around edges and turn out onto plates. Garnish with strawberries, and whipped cream (if using).

VARIATION

Passover Dairy-Free Gluten-Free Flourless Chocolate Lava Cakes

Substitute kosher pareve margarine for the butter, kosher pareve cocoa powder (such as Ghirardelli) for the regular cocoa powder, kosher pareve bittersweet chocolate or semisweet chocolate (such as Lieber's) for the regular chocolate, and kosher nondairy whipped topping for the whipped cream.

NUTRITIONAL INFORMATION, PER SERVING: about 442 cal, 7 g pro, 24 g total fat (13 g sat. fat), 52 g carb, 3 g fibre, 210 mg chol, 93 mg sodium, 287 mg potassium. % RDI: 4% calcium, 21% iron, 17% vit A, 27% vit C, 16% folate.

Flourless Chocolate Truffle Cake

HANDS-ON TIME	TOTAL TIME	MAKES
30 MINUTES	2¾ HOURS	12 SERVINGS

What you need

½ cup	unsalted butter
170 g	bittersweet chocolate, chopped
4	eggs
1 cup	granulated sugar
pinch	salt
⅓ cup	ground almonds
1 tsp	instant espresso powder or instant coffee granules
2 tbsp	cocoa powder

CHOCOLATE ESPRESSO GLAZE:

115 g	bittersweet chocolate, chopped
¼ cup	unsalted butter
¼ cup	hot water
¼ tsp	instant espresso powder

How to make it

Grease then line bottom and side of 9-inch (2.5 L) springform pan with parchment paper. Set aside.

In heatproof bowl over saucepan of hot (not boiling) water, melt butter with chocolate, stirring until smooth. Let cool.

In large bowl, beat together eggs, sugar and salt until pale and thickened, about 5 minutes. Fold in chocolate mixture, almonds and espresso powder. Sift cocoa powder over top; fold in. Scrape into prepared pan, smoothing top.

Bake in 350°F (180°C) oven until crackly on top and cake tester inserted in centre comes out with a few moist crumbs clinging, 30 to 35 minutes. Let cool. Remove side of pan and paper; place cake on rack over rimmed baking sheet.

CHOCOLATE ESPRESSO GLAZE: In heatproof bowl over saucepan of hot (not boiling) water, melt together chocolate, butter, hot water and espresso powder, stirring until smooth. Pour over centre of cake; spread to within 1 inch (2.5 cm) of edge. Refrigerate until set, about 1 hour. *(Make-ahead: Cover loosely and refrigerate for up to 24 hours.)*

VARIATION

Passover Flourless Chocolate Truffle Cake

Substitute kosher pareve margarine for the butter, kosher pareve bittersweet chocolate (such as Lieber's) for the regular chocolate, and kosher pareve cocoa powder (such as Ghirardelli) for the regular cocoa powder.

NUTRITIONAL INFORMATION, PER SERVING: about 345 cal, 4 g pro, 24 g total fat (13 g sat. fat), 30 g carb, 3 g fibre, 93 mg chol, 25 mg sodium, 205 mg potassium. % RDI: 3% calcium, 14% iron, 14% vit A, 5% folate.

Gooey

Chocolate Toffee Squares

HANDS-ON TIME		TOTAL TIME		MAKES
1 HOUR	•	4¼ HOURS	•	ABOUT 96 SQUARES

What you need

1¾ cups	all-purpose flour
¼ cup	granulated sugar
2 tbsp	cornstarch
¼ tsp	salt
1 cup	unsalted butter, softened

TOFFEE FILLING:

1 cup	packed dark brown sugar
1 cup	unsalted butter
1	can (300 mL) sweetened condensed milk
¼ cup	corn syrup

GANACHE TOPPING:

170 g	bittersweet chocolate, chopped
⅔ cup	whipping cream (35%)

How to make it

In food processor, pulse together flour, sugar, cornstarch and salt. Pulse in butter just until mixture holds together. Press evenly into parchment paper–lined 13- x 9-inch (3.5 L) cake pan. Prick all over with fork; refrigerate for 30 minutes.

Bake in 350°F (180°C) oven until light golden, 20 to 25 minutes. Let cool on rack.

TOFFEE FILLING: In saucepan over medium heat, melt together brown sugar, butter, condensed milk and corn syrup, stirring constantly. Reduce heat to medium-low; cook, stirring constantly, until candy thermometer reaches thread stage of 230 to 234°F (110 to 112°C), 25 to 30 minutes, or 1 tsp hot syrup dropped into cold water forms soft 2-inch (5 cm) thread. Pour over base. Refrigerate until cold, about 1 hour.

GANACHE TOPPING: Place chocolate in heatproof bowl. In saucepan, bring cream just to boil; pour over chocolate, whisking until smooth. Let cool to room temperature. Pour over toffee filling, spreading evenly. Refrigerate until set, about 1 hour.

Using parchment paper to lift, transfer to cutting board. Peel paper off sides. Wiping knife with damp cloth between cuts, trim edges even; cut into 1-inch (2.5 cm) squares.

NUTRITIONAL INFORMATION, PER SQUARE: about 84 cal, 1 g pro, 6 g total fat (3 g sat. fat), 9 g carb, trace fibre, 14 mg chol, 14 mg sodium, 28 mg potassium. % RDI: 2% calcium, 1% iron, 4% vit A, 2% folate.

Chocolate-Covered Homemade Marshmallows

HANDS-ON TIME	TOTAL TIME	MAKES
1½ HOURS	7 HOURS	40 PIECES

What you need

⅓ cup	icing sugar
1 cup	granulated sugar
2 tbsp	white corn syrup
2	pkg (each 7 g) unflavoured gelatin
½ cup	cold water
2	egg whites
pinch	salt
¼ tsp	vanilla
225 g	bittersweet chocolate, chopped

How to make it

Grease 9-inch (2.5 L) square cake pan; line with parchment paper. Lightly grease paper; dust with some of the icing sugar. Set aside.

In saucepan, bring granulated sugar, ⅓ cup water and corn syrup to boil over medium-high heat, stirring until sugar is dissolved. Boil, without stirring but brushing down side of pan with pastry brush dipped in cold water, until candy thermometer reaches hard-ball stage of 260°F (125°C), about 12 minutes, or 1 tsp hot syrup dropped into cold water forms hard ball. Remove from heat.

Meanwhile, in saucepan, sprinkle gelatin over cold water; let stand for 5 minutes. Heat over low heat, stirring, until clear, 3 to 5 minutes. Whisk into hot sugar mixture. (Mixture will bubble up.) In stand mixer, beat egg whites with salt until stiff peaks form. With machine running, gradually pour in gelatin mixture, beating on high until increased in volume and cool, 12 minutes. Beat in vanilla.

Immediately scrape into prepared pan. Using greased palette knife or spatula, smooth top. Sprinkle with some of the remaining icing sugar. Let stand, uncovered, at room temperature until firm, about 4 hours.

Remove from pan; peel off paper. Transfer to icing sugar–dusted cutting board. Using greased knife and cleaning and greasing knife between cuts, trim edges even; cut into 40 squares. Gently press sides and bottom of each into remaining icing sugar to coat; dust off excess. Let stand on waxed paper–lined baking sheet until dry, 1 hour. With dry pastry brush, brush off excess sugar.

In heatproof bowl over saucepan of hot (not boiling) water, stir two-thirds of the chocolate just until melted. Remove from heat; stir in remaining chocolate until melted. Using candy-dipping fork or fork, coat each marshmallow in chocolate, tapping fork to let excess chocolate drip back into bowl. Place on parchment paper– or waxed paper–lined baking sheets. Refrigerate until chocolate is firm, about 30 minutes.

NUTRITIONAL INFORMATION, PER PIECE: about 56 cal, 1 g pro, 2 g total fat (1 g sat. fat), 9 g carb, 1 g fibre, 0 mg chol, 5 mg sodium, 2 mg potassium. % RDI: 1% iron.

Chocolate Cinnamon Buns

HANDS-ON TIME	TOTAL TIME	MAKES
1 HOUR	3½ HOURS	15 BUNS

What you need

½ cup	milk
¼ cup	granulated sugar
¼ cup	butter
1 tsp	salt
½ cup	warm water
1 tbsp	active dry yeast
2	eggs, beaten
3½ cups	all-purpose flour (approx)
½ cup	cocoa powder

FILLING:

¾ cup	butter
1 cup	packed brown sugar
½ cup	corn syrup
¾ cup	chopped walnuts or pecans
170 g	bittersweet chocolate, chopped
1 tbsp	cinnamon

How to make it

In saucepan, heat together milk, all but 1 tsp of the sugar, the butter and salt until butter is melted; let cool to lukewarm.

Meanwhile, in large bowl, dissolve remaining sugar in warm water. Sprinkle in yeast; let stand until frothy, about 10 minutes. Stir in eggs and milk mixture.

Into separate bowl, sift flour with cocoa powder; sift again. Gradually beat 1½ cups of the flour mixture into egg mixture until combined; beat for 2 minutes. Stir in enough of the remaining flour mixture to make soft slightly sticky dough that comes away from side of bowl.

Lightly sprinkle some of the remaining flour mixture onto work surface; turn out dough and knead until smooth and elastic, sprinkling with more of the remaining flour mixture if sticky, about 10 minutes. Place in large greased bowl, turning to grease all over. Cover and let rise in warm draft-free place until doubled in bulk, 1 to 1½ hours.

FILLING: In saucepan, melt butter over medium heat; remove 2 tbsp and set aside. Add ¼ cup of the brown sugar and the corn syrup to pan; heat until sugar is dissolved. Pour into greased 13- x 9-inch (3 L) baking dish. Combine remaining brown sugar, walnuts, chocolate and cinnamon; set aside.

Punch down dough. Turn out onto lightly floured surface; roll out into 18- x 14-inch (45 x 35 cm) rectangle. Leaving ½-inch (1 cm) border uncovered, brush with reserved butter; sprinkle with sugar mixture. Starting at long side, tightly roll up, pinching seam to seal. Using serrated knife, cut into 15 pieces; place, cut side down, in prepared pan. Cover and let rise until doubled in bulk, about 1 hour.

Bake in 375°F (190°C) oven until tops sound hollow when tapped, about 25 minutes. Let cool for 3 minutes. Place tray over pan. Wearing oven mitts, grasp pan and tray; turn over. Lift off pan, scraping out remaining filling and drizzling over buns. (*Make-ahead: Cover and store for up to 24 hours. Re-warm in 350°F/180°C oven for about 10 minutes.*)

NUTRITIONAL INFORMATION, PER BUN: about 437 cal, 7 g pro, 24 g total fat (12 g sat. fat), 55 g carb, 4 g fibre, 64 mg chol, 313 mg sodium. % RDI: 5% calcium, 24% iron, 13% vit A, 30% folate.

Rich Double-Chocolate Sauce

HANDS-ON TIME	TOTAL TIME	MAKES
15 MINUTES	45 MINUTES	ABOUT 1½ CUPS

What you need

1 cup	whipping cream (35%)
2 tbsp	corn syrup
115 g	bittersweet chocolate, chopped
55 g	milk chocolate, chopped

How to make it

In small saucepan, bring whipping cream and corn syrup just to boil; remove from heat.

Add bittersweet chocolate and milk chocolate; whisk until smooth. Let cool to room temperature. *(Make-ahead: Refrigerate in airtight container for up to 1 week; gently rewarm to liquefy.)*

TIP FROM THE TEST KITCHEN

Easiest to see on dark bars, bloom is a greyish coating that forms on chocolate when the fat or sugar rises to the surface. This can happen when chocolate is stored in a place that's excessively warm or humid, or as a result of poor tempering. While it may not look attractive, chocolate covered with bloom is perfectly fine to eat.

NUTRITIONAL INFORMATION, PER 1 TBSP: about 76 cal, 1 g pro, 6 g total fat (4 g sat. fat), 5 g carb, 1 g fibre, 13 mg chol, 8 mg sodium. % RDI: 1% calcium, 1% iron, 3% vit A.

Boozy Chocolate Sauce

HANDS-ON TIME	TOTAL TIME	MAKES
10 MINUTES	25 MINUTES	1¾ CUPS

What you need

1 cup	whipping cream (35%)
2 tbsp	corn syrup
170 g	bittersweet chocolate, chopped
2 tbsp	coffee liqueur
1 tbsp	amber rum

How to make it

In saucepan, bring cream and corn syrup to boil; remove from heat. Whisk in chocolate until smooth. Stir in liqueur and rum. Let stand until thickened, about 15 minutes. (*Make-ahead: Refrigerate in airtight container for up to 1 week; gently rewarm to liquefy.*)

NUTRITIONAL INFORMATION, PER 1 TBSP: about 71 cal, 1 g pro, 5 g total fat (3 g sat. fat), 5 g carb, 1 g fibre, 11 mg chol, 5 mg sodium. % RDI: 1% calcium, 2% iron, 3% vit A.

White Chocolate Coconut Sauce

HANDS-ON TIME	TOTAL TIME	MAKES
15 MINUTES	45 MINUTES	ABOUT 2 CUPS

What you need

225 g	white chocolate, chopped
⅔ cup	whipping cream (35%)
½ cup	coconut milk
¼ tsp	coconut extract

How to make it

Place white chocolate in heatproof bowl. In saucepan, bring cream just to boil; pour over chocolate, stirring until smooth. Let cool to room temperature.

Stir in coconut milk and coconut extract. Let cool. (*Make-ahead: Refrigerate in airtight container for up to 3 days; gently rewarm to liquefy.*)

NUTRITIONAL INFORMATION, PER 2 TBSP: about 123 cal, 1 g pro, 10 g total fat (6 g sat. fat), 9 g carb, 0 g fibre, 16 mg chol, 17 mg sodium. % RDI: 3% calcium, 2% iron, 3% vit A, 2% folate.

Gooey

Warm Cinnamon-Chocolate Sauce

HANDS-ON TIME	TOTAL TIME	MAKES
8 MINUTES	8 MINUTES	1⅓ CUPS

What you need

115 g	bittersweet chocolate, chopped
55 g	milk chocolate, chopped
½ cup	milk
2 tbsp	butter
2 tbsp	granulated sugar
2 tbsp	whipping cream (35%)
½ tsp	cinnamon

How to make it

In saucepan, heat together bittersweet chocolate, milk chocolate, milk and butter over-low heat, stirring, until smooth.

Stir in sugar, cream and cinnamon; cook, stirring, until sugar is dissolved, about 1 minute. Let cool for 5 minutes before serving. (Make-ahead: Refrigerate in airtight container for up to 2 weeks; gently rewarm to liquefy.)

NUTRITIONAL INFORMATION, PER 1 TBSP: about 67 cal, 1 g pro, 5 g total fat (3 g sat. fat), 6 g carb, 1 g fibre, 6 mg chol, 14 mg sodium, 59 mg potassium. % RDI: 2% calcium, 5% iron, 2% vit A.

Peanut Butter Caramel Sauce

HANDS-ON TIME	TOTAL TIME	MAKES
15 MINUTES	15 MINUTES	ABOUT 1⅔ CUPS

What you need

¼ cup	unsalted butter
½ cup	packed brown sugar
¼ cup	granulated sugar
¼ cup	golden corn syrup
¼ tsp	salt
⅓ cup	whipping cream (35%)
½ cup	smooth peanut butter

How to make it

In saucepan, melt butter over medium-low heat; stir in brown sugar, granulated sugar, corn syrup, 2 tbsp water and salt. Cook, stirring, until thickened, about 5 minutes.

Stir in cream; cook for 30 seconds. Remove from heat.

Stir in peanut butter; let cool. Serve warm or at room temperature. (Make-ahead: Refrigerate in airtight container for up to 1 week; gently rewarm to liquefy.)

NUTRITIONAL INFORMATION, PER 2 TBSP: about 170 cal, 3 g pro, 10 g total fat (5 g sat. fat), 19 g carb, 1 g fibre, 17 mg chol, 101 mg sodium, 98 mg potassium. % RDI: 1% calcium, 2% iron, 5% vit A, 4% folate.

Rocky Road Cheesecake

HANDS-ON TIME	TOTAL TIME	MAKES
30 MINUTES	8 HOURS	12 SERVINGS

What you need

225 g	bittersweet chocolate or semisweet chocolate, chopped
2	pkg (each 250 g) cream cheese, softened
½ cup	granulated sugar
2	eggs
¾ cup	whipping cream (35%)
2 cups	mini marshmallows
¼ cup	caramel sauce
¼ cup	chocolate sauce

CRUST:

1½ cups	chocolate wafer crumbs
3 tbsp	butter, melted

How to make it

Grease 9-inch (2.5 L) springform pan; line side with parchment paper. Centre on large square of heavy-duty foil; bring foil up and press to side of pan.

CRUST: Stir chocolate wafer crumbs with butter until moistened; press onto bottom of prepared pan. Bake in 325°F (160°C) oven until firm, about 10 minutes. Let cool in pan on rack.

Meanwhile, in heatproof bowl over saucepan of hot (not boiling) water, melt bittersweet chocolate, stirring until smooth; let cool to room temperature.

In large bowl, beat cream cheese until smooth; beat in sugar. Beat in eggs; beat in cream and chocolate until smooth. Scrape over prepared crust; smooth top.

Set pan in larger pan; pour in enough hot water to come 1 inch (2.5 cm) up side. Bake in 325°F (160°C) oven until set around edge but centre is still jiggly, about 1 hour. Turn off oven; let stand in oven for 1 hour.

Transfer springform pan to rack and remove foil; let cool completely. Cover and refrigerate until firm and chilled, about 4 hours. *(Make-ahead: Refrigerate for up to 3 days.)*

Sprinkle marshmallows over cheesecake. Drizzle with caramel and chocolate sauces. *(Make-ahead: Cover with cake dome or loose plastic wrap; refrigerate for up to 4 hours.)*

TIP FROM THE TEST KITCHEN
Use a hot, dry knife to cut cool, creamy cheesecakes into neat slices. Dip the blade into hot water and dry well between slices.

NUTRITIONAL INFORMATION, PER SERVING: about 487 cal, 8 g pro, 36 g total fat (21 g sat. fat), 40 g carb, 4 g fibre, 105 mg chol, 301 mg sodium. % RDI: 7% calcium, 18% iron, 25% vit A, 9% folate.

Milk Chocolate Tart Brûlée

HANDS-ON TIME	TOTAL TIME	MAKES
50 MINUTES	6 HOURS	12 SERVINGS

What you need

⅓ cup	hazelnuts, toasted and skinned
1¼ cups	all-purpose flour
½ cup	unsalted butter, softened
½ cup	granulated sugar
2	egg yolks
pinch	salt

FILLING:

1½ cups	milk
225 g	milk chocolate, chopped
55 g	bittersweet chocolate, chopped
3	eggs
3	egg yolks
½ cup	granulated sugar
1½ tsp	vanilla

TOPPING:

½ cup	granulated sugar
½ cup	whipping cream (35%)
	edible gold flakes

How to make it

In food processor, finely grind hazelnuts with 2 tbsp of the flour; set aside. In bowl, beat butter until light, about 2 minutes. Beat in sugar until fluffy; beat in egg yolks, 1 at a time, beating well after each. Whisk together hazelnut mixture, remaining flour and salt; using wooden spoon, stir into butter mixture until dough holds together, adding up to 2 tbsp water if too crumbly.

Transfer dough to work surface; knead 2 or 3 times to form ball. Press into disc; wrap in plastic wrap and refrigerate until firm, 1 hour. *(Make-ahead: Refrigerate for up to 1 day. Let stand at room temperature for 45 minutes.)*

Press dough onto bottom and up side of greased 11-inch (28 cm) tart pan with removable bottom. Freeze until firm, about 10 minutes. Line pastry shell with foil; fill evenly with pie weights or dried beans. Bake on bottom rack in 400°F (200°C) oven for 20 minutes. Remove weights and foil; bake until golden, about 10 minutes. Let cool in pan on rack.

FILLING: Meanwhile, in saucepan, heat milk until bubbles form around edge. Remove from heat. Whisk in milk chocolate and bittersweet chocolate until smooth. In bowl, whisk together eggs, egg yolks, sugar and vanilla. Gradually whisk in chocolate mixture. Let stand at room temperature for 10 minutes. Pour through fine sieve into prepared tart shell.

Bake in 325°F (160°C) oven just until bubbles rise to surface and knife inserted in centre comes out clean, about 25 minutes. Let cool in pan on rack. Refrigerate until chilled, about 2 hours. *(Make-ahead: Cover loosely with plastic wrap and refrigerate for up to 24 hours.)*

TOPPING: Just before serving, sprinkle sugar evenly over top. Shield crust with strips of foil; using propane torch or under broiler, melt and caramelize sugar. Let stand until sugar is hardened, about 10 minutes. Whip cream; pipe into rosettes or spoon along edge of tart. Garnish with gold flakes.

NUTRITIONAL INFORMATION, PER SERVING: about 505 cal, 9 g pro, 32 g total fat (14 g sat. fat), 51 g carb, 3 g fibre, 171 mg chol, 55 mg sodium. % RDI: 12% calcium, 14% iron, 19% vit A, 20% folate.

White Chocolate Cherry Torte

HANDS-ON TIME	TOTAL TIME	MAKES
30 MINUTES	4½ HOURS	12 SERVINGS

What you need

½ cup	butter, softened
6 tbsp	granulated sugar
1	egg yolk
1 tsp	vanilla
1 cup	all-purpose flour
⅔ cup	ground almonds
pinch	baking powder
¼ cup	sliced almonds, toasted

WHITE CHOCOLATE CUSTARD:

4	egg yolks
2 cups	milk
⅓ cup	granulated sugar
¼ cup	cornstarch
55 g	white chocolate, chopped

BRANDIED CHERRY COMPOTE:

2½ cups	sour cherries, pitted
¼ cup	granulated sugar
2 tsp	cornstarch
2 tbsp	cherry brandy

How to make it

WHITE CHOCOLATE CUSTARD: In bowl, whisk together egg yolks, 1 cup of the milk, sugar and cornstarch. In heavy saucepan, heat remaining milk over medium heat just until bubbles form around edge; gradually whisk into egg mixture. Return to saucepan and cook, whisking, until thick enough to mound on spoon, about 7 minutes. Strain through fine sieve into clean bowl; stir in white chocolate until melted, about 1 minute. Place plastic wrap directly on surface. Refrigerate until cold, about 4 hours. *(Make-ahead: Refrigerate for up to 24 hours.)*

BRANDIED CHERRY COMPOTE: Meanwhile, in saucepan, stir together cherries, sugar and 2 tbsp water over medium-high heat; cook, stirring frequently, until softened, about 15 minutes. Stir cornstarch with 2 tbsp water; stir into cherry mixture and cook, stirring, until thickened, about 1 minute. Stir in cherry brandy. Let cool completely, about 3 hours. *(Make-ahead: Refrigerate in airtight container for up to 24 hours.)*

In large bowl, beat butter with sugar until fluffy; beat in egg yolk and vanilla. Whisk together flour, ground almonds and baking powder; stir into butter mixture to form soft crumbly dough.

Press dough onto bottom and up side of greased 9-inch (23 cm) round tart pan with removable bottom. Refrigerate until firm, about 30 minutes. *(Make-ahead: Cover and refrigerate for up to 24 hours.)*

Using fork, prick crust all over. Line with foil; fill with pie weights or dried beans. Bake in 350°F (180°C) oven until edge starts to turn golden, about 15 minutes. Remove weights and foil; bake until golden, about 15 minutes. Let cool completely in pan on rack.

Fill crust with custard, smoothing top. Top with cherry compote. Sprinkle with almonds.

NUTRITIONAL INFORMATION, PER SERVING: about 312 cal, 6 g pro, 16 g total fat (7 g sat. fat), 37 g carb, 2 g fibre, 104 mg chol, 82 mg sodium, 185 mg potassium. % RDI: 8% calcium, 9% iron, 17% vit A, 3% vit C, 15% folate.

No-Bake Chocolate Marble Cheesecake Pie

HANDS-ON TIME		TOTAL TIME		MAKES
35 MINUTES	•	5¼ HOURS	•	8 TO 10 SERVINGS

What you need

1½ cups	chocolate wafer crumbs
⅓ cup	butter, melted

FILLING:

115 g	bittersweet chocolate, finely chopped
¾ cup	whipping cream (35%)
1½	pkg (each 250 g) cream cheese, softened
⅓ cup	sweetened condensed milk
1 tsp	vanilla

GARNISH:

¾ cup	whipping cream (35%)
30 g	bittersweet chocolate, finely chopped

How to make it

Stir chocolate wafer crumbs with butter until moistened; press onto bottom and up side of 9-inch (23 cm) pie plate. Refrigerate until firm, about 30 minutes.

FILLING: Place chocolate in heatproof bowl. In saucepan, bring half of the cream just to boil; pour over chocolate, whisking until melted and smooth. Let cool slightly.

In separate bowl, beat together cream cheese, remaining cream, sweetened condensed milk and vanilla until smooth; spoon randomly into prepared crust. Pour chocolate mixture into gaps. Using tip of knife, roughly swirl mixtures together. Tap on counter to smooth top. Cover and refrigerate until firm, about 4 hours. *(Make-ahead: Refrigerate for up to 2 days.)*

GARNISH: Whip cream; pipe into rosettes or spoon along edge of pie. Sprinkle chopped chocolate over whipped cream.

NUTRITIONAL INFORMATION, PER EACH OF 10 SERVINGS:
about 482 cal, 7 g pro, 43 g total fat (26 g sat. fat), 24 g carb, 3 g fibre, 110 mg chol, 299 mg sodium. % RDI: 9% calcium, 15% iron, 35% vit A, 8% folate.

Chocolate Peanut Butter Pie

HANDS-ON TIME	TOTAL TIME	MAKES
35 MINUTES	4¾ HOURS	10 SERVINGS

What you need

1½ cups	chocolate wafer crumbs
⅓ cup	butter, melted

FILLING:

½ cup	whipping cream (35%)
1	pkg (250 g) cream cheese, softened
1 cup	smooth natural peanut butter
2 tbsp	butter, softened
1 tbsp	vanilla
1 cup	icing sugar

TOPPING:

55 g	bittersweet chocolate or semisweet chocolate, chopped
3 tbsp	whipping cream (35%)
2 tbsp	chopped roasted peanuts

How to make it

Stir chocolate wafer crumbs with butter until moistened; press onto bottom and up side of 9-inch (23 cm) pie plate. Bake in 350°F (180°C) oven until firm, about 8 minutes. Let cool.

FILLING: Whip cream; set aside. In large bowl, beat cream cheese until smooth; beat in peanut butter, butter and vanilla. Beat in icing sugar until fluffy. Fold in one-quarter of the whipped cream; fold in remaining whipped cream. Spread over prepared crust. Cover loosely and refrigerate until firm, about 2 hours.

TOPPING: Meanwhile, in heatproof bowl set over saucepan of hot (not boiling) water, melt chocolate with cream, stirring until smooth; let cool. Drizzle over filling; sprinkle with peanuts. Cover loosely and refrigerate until set, about 2 hours. (*Make-ahead: Refrigerate for up to 2 days.*)

TIP FROM THE TEST KITCHEN

Natural peanut butter contains only nuts. We use it here and in many other recipes because it has a pure, nutty flavour—and this pie gets plenty of sweetness from the icing sugar in the recipe. If you substitute regular peanut butter in recipes that call for natural, the added sugar and salt will change the flavour.

NUTRITIONAL INFORMATION, PER SERVING: about 521 cal, 11 g pro, 42 g total fat (20 g sat. fat), 31 g carb, 3 g fibre, 75 mg chol, 391 mg sodium. % RDI: 5% calcium, 14% iron, 24% vit A, 15% folate.

Chocolate Fondue

HANDS-ON TIME	TOTAL TIME	MAKES
15 MINUTES	15 MINUTES	2 CUPS

What you need

170 g	bittersweet chocolate, finely chopped
115 g	milk chocolate, finely chopped
¾ cup	whipping cream (35%)
2 tbsp	amaretto, brandy or rum (optional)

How to make it

Place bittersweet chocolate and milk chocolate in shallow heatproof bowl.

In saucepan, bring cream just to boil; pour over chocolate, whisking until melted. Whisk in amaretto (if using).

TIP FROM THE TEST KITCHEN

Serve this fondue in a ceramic fondue pot for entertaining. Avoid metal pots, as they quickly overheat and can scorch the chocolate. For a party, make single batches and refill the pot when it's empty so that the mixture is always fresh. The fondue will stay soft for up to an hour; if it begins to set, microwave it on high for 15 to 20 seconds to reliquefy it.

NUTRITIONAL INFORMATION, PER 1 TBSP: about 64 cal, 1 g pro, 6 g total fat (4 g sat. fat), 4 g carb, 1 g fibre, 8 mg chol, 6 mg sodium. % RDI: 1% calcium, 3% iron, 2% vit A.

Silky Chocolate Mousse

HANDS-ON TIME	TOTAL TIME	MAKES
25 MINUTES	4½ HOURS	6 SERVINGS

What you need

115 g	milk chocolate, chopped
55 g	70% dark chocolate, chopped
1½ cups	whipping cream (35%)
4	egg yolks
3 tbsp	granulated sugar
pinch	salt
½ tsp	vanilla

How to make it

In heatproof bowl over saucepan of hot (not boiling) water, melt milk chocolate with dark chocolate, stirring until smooth. Set aside.

In saucepan, heat ½ cup of the cream over medium-high heat just until tiny bubbles form around edge.

In separate heatproof bowl, whisk together egg yolks, sugar and salt; slowly whisk in hot cream. Place bowl over saucepan of gently simmering water; cook, stirring, until instant-read thermometer reads 160°F (71°C) and custard is thick enough to coat back of spoon, about 15 minutes. Remove from heat.

Whisk in melted chocolate and vanilla. Place plastic wrap directly on surface; let cool for 15 minutes.

Whip remaining cream; fold one-quarter into chocolate mixture. Fold in remaining whipped cream. Divide among dessert dishes; cover and refrigerate until set, about 4 hours. (Make-ahead: Refrigerate for up to 24 hours.)

VARIATION
Silky Mocha Mousse
Heat 2 tbsp instant coffee granules along with cream.

NUTRITIONAL INFORMATION, PER SERVING: about 413 cal, 5 g pro, 34 g total fat (20 g sat. fat), 24 g carb, 2 g fibre, 209 mg chol, 43 mg sodium, 201 mg potassium. % RDI: 9% calcium, 14% iron, 27% vit A, 10% folate.

Chocolate Banana Cream Pie

HANDS-ON TIME	•	TOTAL TIME	•	MAKES
45 MINUTES		6½ HOURS		8 SERVINGS

What you need

1¼ cups	all-purpose flour
½ tsp	salt
¼ cup	cold unsalted butter, cubed
¼ cup	cold lard, cubed
2 tbsp	cold water (approx)
4½ tsp	sour cream
1	egg yolk
45 g	semisweet chocolate, melted
4	bananas, thinly sliced

CUSTARD:

4	egg yolks
2 cups	milk
⅓ cup	granulated sugar
¼ cup	cornstarch
¼ cup	chocolate hazelnut spread (such as Nutella)
1 tsp	vanilla

GARNISH:

½ cup	whipping cream (35%)
2 tsp	granulated sugar
2 tsp	bourbon
1 tsp	vanilla
30 g	semisweet chocolate, shaved

How to make it

In bowl, whisk flour with salt. Using pastry blender or 2 knives, cut in butter and lard until in coarse crumbs with a few larger pieces. Whisk together cold water, sour cream and egg yolk; drizzle over flour mixture, tossing with fork and adding up to 1 tsp more cold water if necessary, until ragged dough forms. Shape into disc; wrap and refrigerate until chilled, about 30 minutes. *(Make-ahead: Refrigerate for up to 3 days or overwrap with foil and freeze for up to 1 month.)*

On lightly floured surface, roll out pastry to generous ⅛-inch (3 mm) thickness; fit into 9-inch (23 cm) pie plate, trimming if necessary to leave ¾-inch (2 cm) overhang. Fold overhang under; crimp edge with fork. Refrigerate for 30 minutes.

Using fork, prick bottom of pastry shell. Line with parchment paper; fill evenly with pie weights or dried beans. Bake on bottom rack in 400°F (200°C) oven until rim is light golden, about 20 minutes. Remove weights and paper; bake until side is golden, about 10 minutes. Let cool in pan on rack.

CUSTARD: In bowl, whisk egg yolks, ½ cup of the milk, sugar and cornstarch. In heavy saucepan, heat remaining milk over medium heat just until bubbles form around edge; gradually whisk into egg yolk mixture. Return to pan and cook, whisking, until thick enough to mound on spoon, about 3 minutes. Strain through fine sieve into bowl; stir in chocolate-hazelnut spread and vanilla. Place plastic wrap directly on surface; refrigerate until cold, about 1 hour. *(Make-ahead: Refrigerate for up to 24 hours.)*

Meanwhile, using pastry brush, paint melted chocolate onto inside of pie shell. Refrigerate until chocolate is firm, 10 minutes. Layer bananas in prepared pie shell; top with custard, smoothing top. Cover and refrigerate for 4 hours.

GARNISH: Whip cream; whisk in sugar, bourbon and vanilla. Leaving 2-inch (5 cm) border, spread over custard. Sprinkle with shaved chocolate.

NUTRITIONAL INFORMATION, PER SERVING: about 498 cal, 8 g pro, 28 g total fat (13 g sat. fat), 56 g carb, 3 g fibre, 153 mg chol, 155 mg sodium, 427 mg potassium. % RDI: 11% calcium, 14% iron, 21% vit A, 8% vit C, 28% folate.

Black Forest Mousse Parfaits

HANDS-ON TIME	TOTAL TIME	MAKES
1¼ HOURS	4½ HOURS	8 SERVINGS

What you need

½ cup	milk
⅓ cup	cocoa powder
55 g	bittersweet chocolate, chopped
3 tbsp	strong brewed coffee or water
⅓ cup	unsalted butter, softened
¾ cup	granulated sugar
2	eggs
1 tsp	vanilla
1 cup	all-purpose flour
½ tsp	each baking soda and baking powder
pinch	salt

WHITE CHOCOLATE MOUSSE:

115 g	white chocolate, chopped
2	eggs
¼ cup	granulated sugar
1¼ cups	whipping cream (35%)

SYRUP:

1	jar (540 mL) pitted sour red cherries in syrup
3 tbsp	kirsch or brandy
2 tbsp	granulated sugar

GARNISH:

30 g	bittersweet chocolate, grated

How to make it

Whisk milk with cocoa powder until smooth; set aside. In heatproof bowl over saucepan of hot (not boiling) water, melt chocolate with coffee, whisking until smooth. In large bowl, beat butter until light, about 1 minute; gradually beat in sugar until fluffy, about 3 minutes. Beat in eggs, 1 at a time; beat in vanilla. Beat in coffee mixture.

Whisk together flour, baking soda, baking powder and salt; stir into butter mixture alternately with cocoa mixture, making 3 additions of flour mixture and 2 of cocoa mixture. Scrape into parchment paper–lined 8-inch (2 L) square cake pan.

Bake in 350°F (180°C) oven until cake tester inserted in centre comes out with a few moist crumbs clinging, 30 to 35 minutes. Let cool in pan on rack. (*Make-ahead: Wrap in plastic wrap and store for up to 24 hours.*)

WHITE CHOCOLATE MOUSSE: In heatproof bowl over saucepan of hot (not boiling) water, melt white chocolate, stirring until smooth; remove from heat. In separate heatproof bowl, whisk eggs with sugar. Place bowl over simmering water; cook, whisking constantly, until thickened and foamy, 4 minutes. Remove from heat; stir in white chocolate. Let cool slightly. Whip cream; fold one-third into white chocolate mixture. Fold in remaining whipped cream; refrigerate until chilled, 2 hours.

SYRUP: Reserving 1¼ cups of the syrup, drain cherries. In saucepan over medium heat, boil syrup until reduced to ¾ cup. Remove from heat; stir in kirsch and sugar. Set aside.

Reserve 8 cherries for garnish. Halve remaining cherries; drain on towel. Fold into mousse. Cut cake into 64 squares. Place 4 squares in each of eight 1-cup (250 mL) glasses, pressing gently; pour 2 tsp of the syrup over top. Top each with ¼ cup of the mousse. Repeat layers once.

GARNISH: Top each with reserved cherry and grated chocolate. (*Make-ahead: Cover; refrigerate for up to 24 hours.*)

NUTRITIONAL INFORMATION, PER SERVING: about 618 cal, 9 g pro, 33 g total fat (19 g sat. fat), 75 g carb, 3 g fibre, 163 mg chol, 168 mg sodium, 308 mg potassium. % RDI: 10% calcium, 21% iron, 31% vit A, 3% vit C, 25% folate.

Classic Chocolate Soufflé

HANDS-ON TIME	TOTAL TIME	MAKES
20 MINUTES	55 MINUTES	8 TO 10 SERVINGS

What you need

⅓ cup	unsalted butter, softened
½ cup	granulated sugar
140 g	bittersweet chocolate, chopped
85 g	milk chocolate, chopped
2 tbsp	brewed coffee or water
pinch	salt
half	vanilla bean (or ¾ tsp vanilla)
2 tbsp	cocoa powder
6	egg yolks
8	egg whites
¼ tsp	cream of tartar
2 tsp	icing sugar or cocoa powder

How to make it

Grease 8- x 3¾-inch (2.5 L) soufflé dish with 4 tsp of the butter; sprinkle with 4 tsp of the granulated sugar, tapping out excess. Wrap parchment paper strip around outside of dish to extend at least 2 inches (5 cm) above rim; tie securely with kitchen string.

In large heatproof bowl over saucepan of hot (not boiling) water, melt together bittersweet chocolate, milk chocolate, coffee, salt and remaining butter, stirring occasionally.

Slit vanilla bean lengthwise; scrape out seeds. Stir seeds into chocolate mixture. Remove from heat; whisk in cocoa powder until smooth. Let cool slightly.

Beat egg yolks with remaining granulated sugar until light and thickened enough that batter falls in ribbons when beaters are lifted, about 2 minutes. Fold into chocolate mixture.

In clean bowl, beat egg whites until foamy; beat in cream of tartar until stiff glossy peaks form. Fold one-quarter into chocolate mixture; fold in remaining egg whites until no streaks remain. Scrape into prepared dish.

Bake on bottom rack in 375°F (190°C) oven until edge is firm and top is lightly browned but centre is still jiggly, 30 to 35 minutes. Sift icing sugar over top. Serve immediately.

NUTRITIONAL INFORMATION, PER EACH OF 10 SERVINGS:
about 273 cal, 6 g pro, 18 g total fat (10 g sat. fat), 24 g carb, 2 g fibre, 141 mg chol, 55 mg sodium, 202 mg potassium. % RDI: 4% calcium, 11% iron, 10% vit A, 8% folate.

Chocolate Hazelnut Trifle

HANDS-ON TIME	TOTAL TIME	MAKES
45 MINUTES	28 HOURS	12 TO 14 SERVINGS

What you need

1	bar (100 g) 70% dark chocolate, cut in ¼-inch (5 mm) pieces
1½ cups	hazelnut liqueur
1¼ cups	whipping cream (35%)
1 tbsp	granulated sugar
¼ cup	chopped skinned toasted hazelnuts
	edible gold leaf (optional)

CUSTARD:

8	egg yolks
4 cups	milk
¾ cup	granulated sugar
½ cup	cornstarch
½ cup	chocolate hazelnut spread (such as Nutella)

CHOCOLATE POUND CAKE:

¾ cup	butter, softened
1 cup	granulated sugar
2	eggs
2 tsp	vanilla
1¾ cups	all-purpose flour
½ cup	cocoa powder, sifted
1 tsp	baking soda
½ tsp	salt
⅔ cup	buttermilk

How to make it

CUSTARD: In large bowl, whisk together egg yolks, ½ cup of the milk, the sugar and cornstarch. In heavy saucepan, heat remaining milk over medium heat just until bubbles form around edge; gradually whisk into yolk mixture. Return to pan and cook, whisking, until thick enough to mound on spoon, about 5 minutes. Strain through fine sieve into clean bowl; stir in chocolate hazelnut spread. Place plastic wrap directly on surface. Refrigerate until cold, 4 hours. *(Make-ahead: Refrigerate for up to 24 hours.)*

CHOCOLATE POUND CAKE: Meanwhile, in bowl, beat butter with sugar until light and fluffy; beat in eggs, 1 at a time. Beat in vanilla. Whisk together flour, cocoa powder, baking soda and salt; stir into butter mixture alternately with buttermilk, making 3 additions of flour mixture and 2 of buttermilk. Spoon into lightly greased 8- x 4-inch (1.5 L) loaf pan, smoothing top.

Bake in 350°F (180°C) oven until cake tester inserted in centre comes out clean, 60 to 70 minutes.

Let cool in pan on rack for 10 minutes. Transfer to rack; let cool completely. *(Make-ahead: Cover and refrigerate for up to 3 days or overwrap in foil and freeze for up to 1 month.)*

Cut cake into ¾-inch (2 cm) cubes. Line 16-cup (4 L) trifle bowl with half of the cake pieces; sprinkle with half of the chocolate. Spoon half of the hazelnut liqueur over top; spread half of the custard over top. Repeat layers once. Cover and refrigerate for 24 hours.

Whip cream with sugar; spread over trifle. Sprinkle with hazelnuts, and gold leaf (if using).

NUTRITIONAL INFORMATION, PER EACH OF 14 SERVINGS: about 615 cal, 10 g pro, 31 g total fat (16 g sat. fat), 73 g carb, 3 g fibre, 203 mg chol, 310 mg sodium, 377 mg potassium. % RDI: 15% calcium, 18% iron, 25% vit A, 26% folate.

Malted Hot Chocolate

HANDS-ON TIME	TOTAL TIME	MAKES
10 MINUTES	10 MINUTES	8 SERVINGS

What you need

8 cups	milk
¼ cup	granulated sugar
⅓ cup	chocolate malt drink mix (such as Ovaltine)
115 g	bittersweet chocolate, finely chopped

How to make it

In saucepan, bring milk and sugar just to boil over medium-high heat, stirring often. Remove from heat.

Whisk in powdered chocolate malt and chopped chocolate until smooth. *(Make-ahead: Let cool. Refrigerate in airtight container for up to 2 days; reheat.)*

NUTRITIONAL INFORMATION, PER SERVING: about 251 cal, 10 g pro, 10 g total fat (6 g sat. fat), 31 g carb, 1 g fibre, 18 mg chol, 122 mg sodium. % RDI: 28% calcium, 5% iron, 12% vit A, 2% vit C, 4% folate.

Marshmallow Hot Chocolate Mix

HANDS-ON TIME	TOTAL TIME	MAKES
5 MINUTES	5 MINUTES	3 CUPS

What you need

2 cups	skim milk powder
¾ cup	instant dissolving (fruit/berry) sugar
½ cup	cocoa powder
1 tsp	cinnamon (optional)
2 cups	mini marshmallows

How to make it

In bowl, stir together skim milk powder, sugar, cocoa powder, and cinnamon (if using). Stir in marshmallows. Spoon into airtight container and seal. *(Make-ahead: Store for up to 1 month.)*

NUTRITIONAL INFORMATION, PER ¼ CUP: about 121 cal, 5 g pro, 1 g total fat (trace sat. fat), 27 g carb, 1 g fibre, 2 mg chol, 67 mg sodium. % RDI: 13% calcium, 4% iron, 8% vit A, 2% vit C, 3% folate.

Chocolate Hazelnut Baklava

HANDS-ON TIME	TOTAL TIME	MAKES
50 MINUTES	1½ HOURS	30 PIECES

What you need

2⅓ cups	hazelnuts
2 tbsp	granulated sugar
½ tsp	cinnamon
¼ tsp	nutmeg
170 g	milk chocolate, chopped
⅔ cup	butter, melted
12	sheets phyllo pastry

SYRUP:

1 cup	granulated sugar
½ cup	liquid honey
1 tbsp	lemon juice

How to make it

Toast hazelnuts on large rimmed baking sheet in 350°F (180°C) oven until fragrant and skins are loose, about 10 minutes. Transfer to tea towel; rub briskly to remove most of the skins. Let cool.

In food processor, chop together hazelnuts, sugar, cinnamon and nutmeg until in coarse crumbs; transfer to bowl. Stir in chocolate; set aside.

Generously brush 13- x 9-inch (3.5 L) cake pan with some of the butter; set aside. Lay phyllo on work surface with short end facing you.

Cut stack in half crosswise; stack halves together and cover with damp towel to prevent drying out. Place 1 sheet of phyllo on work surface; brush lightly with some of the butter. Top with second sheet of phyllo; brush with butter. Repeat layers with 4 more sheets.

Place buttered phyllo stack in prepared pan; sprinkle with 1 cup of the hazelnut mixture. Stack 4 more phyllo sheets, brushing each lightly with some of the butter; place on hazelnut mixture in pan. Sprinkle with 1 cup of the remaining hazelnut mixture. Repeat layers twice, using 8 sheets buttered phyllo and remaining hazelnut mixture. Stack remaining 6 phyllo sheets, brushing each with some of the remaining butter. Place on top of layers in pan; press gently to compact slightly.

Using tip of sharp knife and without cutting all the way through to filling, score top into squares or diamonds. Bake in 350°F (180°C) oven until phyllo is golden, crisp and flaky, 40 to 45 minutes.

SYRUP: Meanwhile, in small saucepan, whisk together sugar, honey, ⅓ cup water and lemon juice. Bring to boil over medium-high heat; boil, stirring, for 1 minute. Pour over hot baklava. Let cool in pan on rack. Cut along score lines into pieces. (Make-ahead: Store in airtight container for up to 24 hours.)

NUTRITIONAL INFORMATION, PER PIECE: about 207 cal, 3 g pro, 13 g total fat (4 g sat. fat), 22 g carb, 2 g fibre, 14 mg chol, 94 mg sodium. % RDI: 3% calcium, 6% iron, 4% vit A, 7% folate.

Cranberry White Chocolate Biscotti

HANDS-ON TIME	TOTAL TIME	MAKES
25 MINUTES	1½ HOURS	ABOUT 36 COOKIES

What you need

½ cup	butter, softened
1 cup	granulated sugar
2	eggs
1 tsp	vanilla
2½ cups	all-purpose flour
2 tsp	baking powder
¼ tsp	salt
1 cup	shelled pistachios
1 cup	dried cranberries
1	egg white
280 g	white chocolate, melted

How to make it

In large bowl, beat butter with sugar until fluffy; beat in eggs, 1 at a time. Beat in vanilla. Whisk together flour, baking powder and salt; add to butter mixture in 2 additions, stirring just until combined. Stir in pistachios and cranberries.

Divide dough in half. On lightly floured surface, shape each half into 12-inch (30 cm) long rectangle. Place, 2 inches (5 cm) apart, on parchment paper–lined rimless baking sheet; press to flatten slightly. Stir egg white with 1 tsp water; liberally brush over tops of biscotti.

Bake in 325°F (160°C) oven until light golden and just firm to the touch, about 30 minutes. Let cool on pan on rack for 10 minutes.

Transfer logs to cutting board. Using chef's knife, cut diagonally into ½-inch (1 cm) thick slices. Stand slices upright, about ½ inch (1 cm) apart, on baking sheet. Bake in 300°F (150°C) oven until almost dry, about 35 minutes. Transfer to rack; let cool completely.

Dip 1 end of each biscotti in white chocolate, letting excess drip off. Place on waxed paper– or parchment paper–lined baking sheet; refrigerate until chocolate is set, about 20 minutes.

NUTRITIONAL INFORMATION, PER COOKIE: about 130 cal, 2 g pro, 5 g total fat (3 g sat. fat), 19 g carb, 1 g fibre, 17 mg chol, 64 mg sodium, 38 mg potassium. % RDI: 2% calcium, 4% iron, 3% vit A, 9% folate.

Tropical Fruit Bark

HANDS-ON TIME	TOTAL TIME	MAKES
15 MINUTES	1¼ HOURS	50 PIECES

What you need

450 g	white chocolate, chopped
½ cup	chopped macadamia nuts
½ cup	diced dried mango
½ cup	diced dried papaya
½ cup	diced candied pineapple

How to make it

Line rimmed baking sheet with parchment paper; draw 12- x 8-inch (30 x 20 cm) rectangle on paper. Turn paper over.

In bowl over saucepan of hot (not boiling) water, melt white chocolate, stirring occasionally until smooth. Remove from heat; stir in macadamia nuts, mango, papaya and pineapple. Spread evenly onto rectangle on paper.

Refrigerate until firm, about 1 hour. Break into pieces. *(Make-ahead: Layer between waxed paper in airtight container and refrigerate for up to 2 weeks.)*

VARIATION
Black Forest Bark
Omit white chocolate. Melt 450 g semisweet chocolate or bittersweet chocolate as directed. Omit macadamia nuts and dried fruit; add 2 cups dried sour cherries or cranberries.

NUTRITIONAL INFORMATION, PER PIECE: about 73 cal, 1 g pro, 4 g total fat (2 g sat. fat), 9 g carb, trace fibre, 2 mg chol, 9 mg sodium. % RDI: 2% calcium, 1% iron, 2% vit A, 7% vit C, 1% folate.

Bittersweet Amaretti Bark

HANDS-ON TIME	TOTAL TIME	MAKES
15 MINUTES	45 MINUTES	16 PIECES

What you need

450 g	bittersweet chocolate, melted
1 cup	quartered amaretti cookies
1 tsp	vanilla

How to make it

Line 15- x 10-inch (38 x 25 cm) rimmed baking sheet with foil; grease foil. Set aside.

In large bowl, stir together chocolate, amaretti cookies and vanilla. Spread to about ¼-inch (5 mm) thickness over two-thirds of prepared pan. Refrigerate until firm, about 30 minutes.

Break bark into chunks. *(Make-ahead: Layer between waxed paper in airtight container and refrigerate for up to 2 weeks.)*

NUTRITIONAL INFORMATION, PER PIECE: about 176 cal, 2 g pro, 11 g total fat (6 g sat. fat), 18 g carb, 2 g fibre, 0 mg chol, 9 mg sodium. % RDI: 2% calcium, 9% iron.

Marbled Almond Bark

HANDS-ON TIME	TOTAL TIME	MAKES
25 MINUTES	1½ HOURS	50 PIECES

What you need

225 g	semisweet chocolate, chopped
2 cups	natural almonds, toasted
225 g	white chocolate, chopped

How to make it

Line rimmed baking sheet with parchment paper; draw 12- x 8-inch (30 x 20 cm) rectangle on paper. Turn paper over.

In bowl over saucepan of hot (not boiling) water, melt semisweet chocolate, stirring occasionally until smooth. Remove from heat; stir in almonds. Spread evenly onto rectangle on paper.

In bowl over saucepan of hot (not boiling) water, melt white chocolate, stirring occasionally until smooth. Spoon over semisweet chocolate; swirl with tip of knife. Refrigerate until firm, about 1 hour. Break into pieces. *(Make-ahead: Layer between waxed paper in airtight container and refrigerate for up to 2 weeks.)*

NUTRITIONAL INFORMATION, PER PIECE: about 79 cal, 2 g pro, 6 g total fat (2 g sat. fat), 7 g carb, 1 g fibre, 0 mg chol, 5 mg sodium, 71 mg potassium. % RDI: 2% calcium, 3% iron, 1% folate.

Hazelnut Chocolate Pizzelle

HANDS-ON TIME	TOTAL TIME	MAKES
30 MINUTES	50 MINUTES	12 COOKIES

What you need

⅓ cup	hazelnuts
⅓ cup	butter
½ cup	granulated sugar
2	eggs
1 tbsp	hazelnut liqueur
1 cup	all-purpose flour
½ cup	cocoa powder
1 tsp	baking powder

How to make it

On rimmed baking sheet, toast hazelnuts in 350°F (180°C) oven until fragrant and skins are loose, about 15 minutes. Transfer to tea towel; rub briskly to remove as much of the skins as possible. Let cool. In food processor or using knife, chop finely. Set aside.

In saucepan over medium heat or in microwave, melt butter. Whisk in sugar, then eggs, 1 at a time; whisk in hazelnut liqueur.

Whisk together flour, cocoa powder and baking powder. Add to egg mixture; stir until smooth. Stir in hazelnuts to form stiff but sticky batter.

Preheat pizzelle iron over medium heat. Spoon heaping 2 tbsp batter into centre; close lid and lock handles. Cook, turning iron once, until pizzelle is crisp and pulls away easily from iron, about 45 seconds.

Using fork to lift edge, transfer to rack. Let cool; trim excess from around edge. Repeat with remaining batter. *(Make-ahead: Let cool completely. Divide in 2 stacks; wrap each in plastic wrap. Store in airtight container for up to 3 days or freeze for up to 3 weeks.)*

TIP FROM THE TEST KITCHEN

If pizzelle are soft after thawing, place in single layer on rimmed baking sheet; bake in 300°F (150°C) oven until crisp, about 5 minutes.

NUTRITIONAL INFORMATION, PER COOKIE: about 165 cal, 3 g pro, 9 g total fat (4 g sat. fat), 20 g carb, 2 g fibre, 47 mg chol, 85 mg sodium. % RDI: 2% calcium, 9% iron, 6% vit A, 10% folate.

Chocolate Hazelnut Palmiers

HANDS-ON TIME	TOTAL TIME	MAKES
40 MINUTES	2¼ HOURS	48 PIECES

What you need

½ cup	hazelnuts
115 g	semisweet chocolate, melted
1	egg yolk

QUICK PUFF PASTRY:

1 cup	cold unsalted butter, cubed
1⅔ cups	all-purpose flour
¾ tsp	salt
⅓ cup	cold water

How to make it

QUICK PUFF PASTRY: Set aside three-quarters of the butter in refrigerator. In food processor, blend flour with salt. Sprinkle remaining butter over top; pulse until indistinguishable, 10 seconds. Sprinkle with reserved butter; pulse 4 or 5 times or until in pea-size pieces.

Pour cold water evenly over mixture (not through feed tube). Pulse 6 to 8 times until loose ragged dough forms (do not let form ball). Transfer to floured waxed paper; press into rectangle. Dust with flour; top with waxed paper. Roll out into 15- x 12-inch (38 x 30 cm) rectangle.

Remove top paper. Starting at long edge and using bottom paper to lift pastry, fold over one-third; fold opposite long edge over top, bringing flush with edge of first fold to make 15- x 4-inch (38 x 10 cm) rectangle. Starting from 1 short end, roll up firmly; flatten into 5-inch (12 cm) square. Wrap and refrigerate until firm, about 1 hour. (Make-ahead: Refrigerate in airtight container for up to 5 days or freeze for up to 2 weeks.)

In cake pan, toast hazelnuts in 350°F (180°C) oven until fragrant and skins crack, 10 minutes. Transfer to towel; rub to remove as much skin as possible. Finely chop nuts.

Divide pastry in half. On lightly floured surface, roll out each half into 10-inch (25 cm) square. Leaving ½-inch (1 cm) border on all sides, brush with chocolate. Sprinkle with hazelnuts. Starting at 1 end, roll up to centre of square; roll up opposite end to meet in centre. Arrange rolls, seam side down, on parchment paper–lined baking sheets. Cover and freeze until firm, about 15 minutes.

Transfer rolls to cutting board. In bowl, beat egg yolk with 1 tbsp water; brush over rolls. Using serrated knife, trim ends even; cut each roll into twenty-four ¼-inch (5 mm) thick slices. (Make-ahead: Layer between waxed paper in airtight container; freeze for up to 2 weeks. Bake from frozen, adding 5 minutes to baking time.) Return, cut sides down, to baking sheets. Bake in 450°F (230°C) oven until puffed and golden, about 12 minutes.

NUTRITIONAL INFORMATION, PER PIECE: about 73 cal, 1 g pro, 6 g total fat (3 g sat. fat), 5 g carb, trace fibre, 15 mg chol, 37 mg sodium. % RDI: 2% iron, 4% vit A, 5% folate.

Toffee Chocolate Chip Toonies

HANDS-ON TIME	TOTAL TIME	MAKES
30 MINUTES	50 MINUTES	ABOUT 75 COOKIES

What you need

⅔ cup	unsalted butter, softened
¾ cup	packed brown sugar
¼ cup	granulated sugar
1	egg
1 tsp	vanilla
1⅔ cups	all-purpose flour
½ tsp	baking soda
¼ tsp	salt
½ cup	toffee bits
½ cup	mini semisweet chocolate chips

How to make it

In large bowl, beat together butter, brown sugar and granulated sugar until fluffy; beat in egg and vanilla.

Whisk together flour, baking soda and salt; stir into butter mixture until combined. Stir in toffee bits and chocolate chips.

Drop by rounded 1 tsp, about 2 inches (5 cm) apart, onto parchment paper–lined rimless baking sheets. Bake in 350°F (180°C) oven until golden, 10 to 12 minutes.

Let cool on pan on rack for 5 minutes. Transfer to rack; let cool completely.

TIP FROM THE TEST KITCHEN

A scoop with a pusher in it (like an ice cream scoop) is a handy tool for cookie baking. Scoops come in a range of sizes— from small for dainty cookies to extra-large for muffins—and speed up the dough-dropping process.

NUTRITIONAL INFORMATION, PER COOKIE: about 47 cal, trace pro, 2 g total fat (2 g sat. fat), 6 g carb, trace fibre, 8 mg chol, 23 mg sodium, 16 mg potassium. % RDI: 1% iron, 2% vit A, 3% folate.

Triple-Chocolate Cookies

HANDS-ON TIME
35 MINUTES

TOTAL TIME
35 MINUTES

MAKES
ABOUT 48 COOKIES

What you need

1 cup	butter, softened
1 cup	granulated sugar
½ cup	packed brown sugar
2	eggs
1 tsp	vanilla
2¼ cups	all-purpose flour
½ cup	cocoa powder
1 tsp	baking soda
¼ tsp	salt
170 g	bittersweet chocolate, chopped
115 g	milk chocolate, chopped
1 cup	coarsely chopped walnuts (optional)

How to make it

In large bowl, beat together butter, granulated sugar and brown sugar until fluffy. Beat in eggs, 1 at a time; beat in vanilla. Sift together flour, cocoa powder, baking soda and salt; stir into butter mixture. Stir in bittersweet and milk chocolates, and walnuts (if using).

Drop by heaping 1 tbsp, about 2 inches (5 cm) apart, onto parchment paper–lined rimless baking sheets. Bake on top and bottom racks in 350°F (180°C) oven, rotating and switching pans halfway through, until firm to the touch and no longer glossy, about 12 minutes.

Let cool on pans on racks for 2 minutes. Transfer to racks; let cool completely. *(Make-ahead: Layer between waxed paper in airtight container and store for up to 3 days or freeze for up to 2 weeks.)*

NUTRITIONAL INFORMATION, PER COOKIE: about 117 cal, 2 g pro, 6 g total fat (4 g sat. fat), 15 g carb, 1 g fibre, 18 mg chol, 71 mg sodium. % RDI: 1% calcium, 5% iron, 4% vit A, 6% folate.

Malted
Hot Chocolate
page 45

Triple-Chocolate
Cookies
opposite

Chocolate Overload Cookies

HANDS-ON TIME	TOTAL TIME	MAKES
25 MINUTES	2¾ HOURS	ABOUT 30 COOKIES

What you need

¾ cup	unsalted butter, softened
⅓ cup	each granulated sugar and packed brown sugar
1 tsp	vanilla
1	egg
1½ cups	all-purpose flour
½ cup	cocoa powder
½ tsp	baking powder
¼ tsp	each baking soda and salt
⅓ cup	each chopped bittersweet chocolate, milk chocolate and white chocolate

How to make it

In large bowl, beat together butter, granulated sugar and brown sugar; beat in vanilla and egg.

Sift together flour, cocoa powder, baking powder, baking soda and salt; stir into butter mixture. Stir in bittersweet chocolate, milk chocolate and white chocolate. Form into 10-inch (25 cm) long log; wrap and refrigerate until firm, about 2 hours.

Using sawing motion with sharp knife, cut log into generous ¼-inch (5 mm) thick slices. Place, 1 inch (2.5 cm) apart, on parchment paper–lined rimless baking sheets.

Bake in 350°F (180°C) oven until firm, 10 to 11 minutes. Let cool on pans on racks for 5 minutes. Transfer to racks; let cool completely.

NUTRITIONAL INFORMATION, PER COOKIE: about 48 cal, 1 g pro, 3 g total fat (2 g sat. fat), 5 g carb, trace fibre, 8 mg chol, 18 mg sodium, 13 mg potassium. % RDI: 1% calcium, 1% iron, 2% vit A, 3% folate.

Cocoa Sugar Cookies

HANDS-ON TIME	TOTAL TIME	MAKES
30 MINUTES	2 HOURS	ABOUT 24 COOKIES

What you need

¾ cup	unsalted butter, softened
1 cup	granulated sugar
1	egg
1 tsp	vanilla
2¼ cups	all-purpose flour
⅓ cup	cocoa powder
½ tsp	baking powder
¼ tsp	salt

How to make it

In bowl, beat butter with sugar until fluffy; beat in egg and vanilla. Whisk flour, cocoa powder, baking powder and salt; stir into butter mixture in 2 additions. Divide in half; flatten into discs. Wrap and refrigerate until firm, about 1 hour. (Make-ahead: Refrigerate for up to 24 hours.)

On floured surface, roll out each disc to ¼-inch (5 mm) thickness. Using cookie cutter, cut out desired shapes, rerolling scraps and chilling dough before cutting again. Place, 1 inch (2.5 cm) apart, on parchment paper–lined rimless baking sheets. Freeze for 15 minutes or refrigerate for 30 minutes until firm.

Bake in 350°F (180°C) oven until edges begin to darken, 20 to 25 minutes. Let cool on pans on racks for 2 minutes. Transfer to racks; let cool completely. (Make-ahead: Store in airtight container for up to 1 month.)

NUTRITIONAL INFORMATION, PER COOKIE: about 132 cal, 2 g pro, 6 g total fat (4 g sat. fat), 18 g carb, 1 g fibre, 23 mg chol, 34 mg sodium. % RDI: 1% calcium, 6% iron, 5% vit A, 11% folate.

Chocolate Macarons

HANDS-ON TIME	TOTAL TIME	MAKES
35 MINUTES	1¼ HOURS	ABOUT 30 COOKIES

What you need

1 cup	icing sugar
½ cup	ground almonds
2 tbsp	cocoa powder
2	egg whites
2 tbsp	granulated sugar
1½ tsp	meringue powder

BLACK CURRANT FILLING:

1 cup	black currant jam

How to make it

In food processor, pulse together icing sugar, almonds and cocoa powder until fine. Sift through fine sieve into bowl; set aside. In large bowl, beat egg whites until foamy. Beat in granulated sugar and meringue powder until soft peaks form. Fold in almond mixture, one-third at a time, until blended.

Using piping bag fitted with ¼-inch (5 mm) plain tip, pipe meringue into 1-inch (2.5 cm) rounds, 1 inch (2.5 cm) apart, on parchment paper–lined rimless baking sheets. Let stand for 15 minutes.

Bake in 325°F (160°C) oven until puffed, smooth on top and cracked around bottom edges, 12 to 14 minutes. Let cool on pans on racks. *(Make-ahead: Store in airtight container for up to 3 days.)*

BLACK CURRANT FILLING: Meanwhile, press jam through fine sieve into small saucepan. Bring to boil over medium heat; reduce heat and simmer until thickened slightly, about 5 minutes. Transfer to bowl; let cool, stirring occasionally, until thickened and spreadable.

Spread about ¼ tsp filling onto bottom of each of half of the macarons. Sandwich with remaining macarons, bottom side down. *(Make-ahead: Layer between waxed paper in airtight container and store for up to 24 hours.)*

VARIATION

Chocolate Ganache Macarons

Omit black currant filling. In saucepan, heat ¼ cup whipping cream (35%) over medium heat until small bubbles form around edge. Stir in 55 g bittersweet chocolate, finely chopped, until melted. Stir in 1 tbsp unsalted butter until smooth. Transfer to bowl. Let cool until thick enough to spread. Fill and sandwich cookies as directed.

NUTRITIONAL INFORMATION, PER COOKIE: about 59 cal, 1 g pro, 1 g total fat (trace sat. fat), 12 g carb, trace fibre, 0 mg chol, 7 mg sodium, 23 mg potassium. % RDI: 1% calcium, 1% iron, 2% vit C, 2% folate.

Chocolate Babka

HANDS-ON TIME	TOTAL TIME	MAKES
35 MINUTES	4¾ HOURS	2 LOAVES, 8 SLICES EACH

What you need

¾ cup	2% milk or homogenized milk
1	pkg (8 g) active dry yeast (or 2¼ tsp)
⅓ cup	granulated sugar
⅓ cup	unsalted butter, softened
¾ tsp	salt
3	eggs
3¼ cups	all-purpose flour (approx)

FILLING:

¼ cup	unsalted butter, softened
½ cup	granulated sugar
½ cup	cocoa powder

STREUSEL:

⅓ cup	all-purpose flour
¼ cup	granulated sugar
3 tbsp	unsalted butter

How to make it

In saucepan, heat milk over medium-low heat just until warm to the touch (100°F/38°C); pour into large bowl. Sprinkle in yeast; let stand until frothy, about 10 minutes.

Transfer to stand mixer. Whisk in sugar, butter, salt and 2 of the eggs. Add 3 cups of the flour; mix, adding remaining flour, 1 tbsp at a time, if necessary, until dough is smooth, elastic and comes away from side of bowl, about 10 minutes. Transfer to lightly floured surface; knead into ball. Place in large greased bowl, turning to grease all over. Cover and let rise in warm place until doubled in bulk, about 1½ hours.

Punch down dough; divide in half. Roll out each half into 18- x 7-inch (45 x 18 cm) rectangle.

FILLING: Leaving ½-inch (1 cm) border on 1 long side of each, spread butter over rectangles. Mix sugar with cocoa powder; sprinkle over butter. Starting at long buttered side, roll up tightly into log; pinch edge to seal, brushing with water if necessary. Fold each log in half; twist twice and pinch open ends together to seal. Fit into 2 greased 8- x 4-inch (1.5 L) loaf pans. Cover with greased plastic wrap; let rise in warm place until doubled in bulk, 1 to 1½ hours. Whisk remaining egg with 2 tsp water. Brush over loaves.

STREUSEL: Stir flour with sugar. Using pastry blender or 2 knives, cut in butter until in coarse crumbs. Sprinkle over loaves.

Bake in 350°F (180°C) oven until browned and bottoms sound hollow when tapped, 35 to 40 minutes. Transfer to racks; let cool.

NUTRITIONAL INFORMATION, PER SLICE: about 257 cal, 5 g pro, 11 g total fat (6 g sat. fat), 37 g carb, 2 g fibre, 59 mg chol, 126 mg sodium, 138 mg potassium. % RDI: 3% calcium, 14% iron, 10% vit A, 33% folate.

Chocolate Breakfast Braid

HANDS-ON TIME	TOTAL TIME	MAKES
45 MINUTES	4¾ HOURS	2 LOAVES, 12 SLICES EACH

What you need

1½ cups	chopped bittersweet chocolate or milk chocolate (about 210 g)
1	egg, beaten

SWEET YEAST DOUGH:

¼ cup	granulated sugar
¼ cup	warm water
1	pkg (8 g) active dry yeast (or 2¼ tsp)
½ cup	milk
¼ cup	butter
1 tsp	salt
2	eggs, beaten
4 cups	all-purpose flour (approx)

How to make it

SWEET YEAST DOUGH: In large bowl, stir 2 tsp of the sugar with warm water until dissolved. Sprinkle in yeast; let stand until frothy, about 10 minutes.

Meanwhile, in saucepan, heat milk, remaining sugar, butter and salt until butter is melted; let cool to lukewarm. Stir into yeast mixture along with eggs. Stir in 3¼ cups of the flour, about 1 cup at a time, to form shaggy dough.

Turn out onto lightly floured surface; knead, adding as much of the remaining flour as necessary, until smooth and elastic, about 10 minutes. Transfer to large greased bowl, turning to grease all over. Cover and let rise in warm draft-free place until doubled in bulk, about 1½ hours.

Punch down dough; divide in half. Working with half at a time, divide dough into thirds. Press or roll each third into 8- x 4-inch (20 x 10 cm) rectangle. Leaving 1-inch (2.5 cm) border all around, sprinkle ¼ cup of the chocolate onto centre of each. Fold long sides of dough together, pinching to enclose chocolate. Roll each gently into rope about 12 inches (30 cm) long.

Pinch 3 ropes together at 1 end. Braid ropes, pinching ends and tucking under. Repeat with remaining dough to make second loaf. Place loaves, 3 inches (8 cm) apart, on parchment paper–lined or greased large baking sheet. *(Make-ahead: Cover and refrigerate for up to 12 hours; let come to room temperature before continuing, about 40 minutes.)* Cover and let rise in warm draft-free place until doubled in bulk, about 1 hour.

Brush tops with egg. Bake in 375°F (190°C) oven until golden and loaves sound hollow when tapped on bottoms, about 20 minutes. Let cool on pan on rack for 5 minutes. Transfer to rack; let cool completely. *(Make-ahead: Wrap in plastic wrap and overwrap in heavy-duty foil; freeze for up to 2 weeks.)*

NUTRITIONAL INFORMATION, PER SLICE: about 157 cal, 4 g pro, 7 g total fat (4 g sat. fat), 21 g carb, 2 g fibre, 29 mg chol, 121 mg sodium. % RDI: 2% calcium, 11% iron, 3% vit A, 25% folate.

Chocolate Bar Brownies

HANDS-ON TIME	TOTAL TIME	MAKES
30 MINUTES	1½ HOURS	ABOUT 40 BARS

What you need

⅔ cup	butter
210 g	bittersweet chocolate, chopped
140 g	unsweetened chocolate, chopped
1½ cups	granulated sugar
2 tsp	vanilla
4	eggs
1 cup	all-purpose flour
1 tsp	salt

TOPPING:

140 g	bittersweet chocolate, chopped
⅔ cup	whipping cream (35%)
1 cup	chopped chocolate-covered candy (such as Turtles, Maltesers, After Eights or Rolos)

How to make it

In saucepan, melt together butter, bittersweet chocolate and unsweetened chocolate over medium-low heat, stirring until smooth; let cool for 10 minutes.

Whisk in sugar and vanilla; whisk in eggs, 1 at a time. Stir in flour and salt. Spread in parchment paper–lined 13- x 9-inch (3.5 L) cake pan; smooth top.

Bake in 350°F (180°C) oven until cake tester inserted in centre comes out with a few moist crumbs clinging, about 25 minutes. Let cool in pan on rack.

TOPPING: Place bittersweet chocolate in heatproof bowl. In saucepan, bring cream just to boil; pour over bittersweet chocolate, whisking until smooth. Let cool for 3 minutes. Spread over brownies; sprinkle with candy. Cut into bars.

TIP FROM THE TEST KITCHEN

Pure vanilla extract—not artificial— is made by percolating vanilla beans with ethyl alcohol and water, and its pure flavour is vital in custards and delicate, fresh desserts. Artificial, or imitation, vanilla extract does have its uses, though. It works well in high heat and can taste just fine in longer-baked cakes or loaves.

NUTRITIONAL INFORMATION, PER BAR: about 182 cal, 2 g pro, 11 g total fat (7 g sat. fat), 18 g carb, 1 g fibre, 37 mg chol, 103 mg sodium. % RDI: 2% calcium, 6% iron, 6% vit A, 4% folate.

The Best Chocolate Brownies

HANDS-ON TIME	•	TOTAL TIME	•	MAKES
20 MINUTES		4 HOURS		48 BARS

What you need

225 g	bittersweet chocolate, chopped
55 g	unsweetened chocolate, chopped
1 cup	butter
2 cups	granulated sugar
1 tbsp	vanilla
4	eggs
1 cup	all-purpose flour
¼ tsp	salt

How to make it

In saucepan, melt together bittersweet chocolate, unsweetened chocolate and butter over medium-low heat, stirring occasionally; let cool for 10 minutes.

Whisk in sugar and vanilla; whisk in eggs, 1 at a time. With wooden spoon, stir in flour and salt. Spread in greased or parchment paper–lined 13- x 9-inch (3 L) baking dish; smooth top.

Bake in 350°F (180°C) oven until cake tester inserted in centre comes out with a few moist crumbs clinging, 35 to 40 minutes.

Let cool in pan on rack. Cut into bars. (Make-ahead: Layer between waxed paper in airtight container and refrigerate for up to 3 days or freeze for up to 2 weeks.)

TIP FROM THE TEST KITCHEN

It can be a challenge to line square and rectangular pans with parchment paper. Here's the Test Kitchen's foolproof method: Place the pan on a large sheet of parchment paper; cut the paper 3 inches (8 cm) larger than the bottom of the pan on each side. At each corner of the paper, make a 3-inch (8 cm) long cut from the corner toward the centre. Lightly grease the pan; place the paper in the pan, pressing the bottom to adhere. At each corner, tuck one cut strip of paper behind the other; add batter.

NUTRITIONAL INFORMATION, PER BAR: about 115 cal, 1 g pro, 7 g total fat (4 g sat. fat), 13 g carb, 1 g fibre, 26 mg chol, 45 mg sodium, 46 mg potassium. % RDI: 1% calcium, 5% iron, 4% vit A, 4% folate.

Peanut Butter Brownies

HANDS-ON TIME	TOTAL TIME	MAKES
30 MINUTES	2½ HOURS	60 BARS

What you need

170 g	bittersweet chocolate, chopped
115 g	unsweetened chocolate, chopped
⅓ cup	butter
⅓ cup	smooth natural peanut butter, at room temperature
2 cups	granulated sugar
1 tsp	vanilla
4	eggs
1⅔ cups	all-purpose flour
1 cup	chopped unsalted peanuts
pinch	salt

TOPPING:

⅓ cup	butter, softened
¼ cup	smooth natural peanut butter, at room temperature
½ tsp	vanilla
2 cups	icing sugar
1 tbsp	milk
85 g	bittersweet chocolate, melted

How to make it

In saucepan, melt together bittersweet chocolate, unsweetened chocolate, butter and peanut butter over medium-low heat, stirring until smooth; let cool for 10 minutes. Whisk in sugar and vanilla. Whisk in eggs, 1 at a time, whisking well after each. Stir in flour, peanuts and salt. Spread in parchment paper–lined or greased 13- x 9-inch (3.5 L) cake pan.

Bake in 350°F (180°C) oven until cake tester inserted in centre comes out with a few moist crumbs clinging, about 25 minutes. Let cool in pan on rack.

TOPPING: In bowl, beat together butter, peanut butter and vanilla until creamy. Beat in icing sugar in 2 additions; beat in milk. Using paper as handles, transfer brownies to cutting board; peel off paper. Spread peanut butter mixture over brownies. Drizzle with melted chocolate.

Wrap in plastic wrap and refrigerate until firm, about 1 hour. *(Make-ahead: Refrigerate for up to 5 days or overwrap in heavy-duty foil and freeze for up to 1 month.)*

Cut into bars.

NUTRITIONAL INFORMATION, PER BAR: about 139 cal, 3 g pro, 7 g total fat (3 g sat. fat), 17 g carb, 1 g fibre, 18 mg chol, 20 mg sodium. % RDI: 1% calcium, 4% iron, 2% vit A, 5% folate.

Monkey Bars

HANDS-ON TIME	TOTAL TIME	MAKES
12 MINUTES	2 HOURS	25 BARS

What you need

1½ cups	chocolate wafer crumbs
⅓ cup	butter, melted
1½ cups	banana chips, broken in pieces
1 cup	semisweet chocolate chips
1 cup	salted roasted peanuts
¾ cup	peanut butter chips
1	can (300 mL) sweetened condensed milk

How to make it

Stir chocolate wafer crumbs with butter until moistened; press into parchment paper–lined 9-inch (2.5 L) square cake pan.

Sprinkle with banana chips, chocolate chips, peanuts and peanut butter chips; pour sweetened condensed milk over top.

Bake in 350°F (180°C) oven until set in centre, about 30 minutes. Let cool in pan on rack for 30 minutes.

Cover and refrigerate until completely cool, about 1 hour. *(Make-ahead: Remove from pan; wrap in plastic wrap and refrigerate for up to 5 days or overwrap in foil and freeze for up to 1 month.)*

Cut into bars.

NUTRITIONAL INFORMATION, PER BAR: about 216 cal, 5 g pro, 13 g total fat (6 g sat. fat), 23 g carb, 2 g fibre, 12 mg chol, 112 mg sodium, 176 mg potassium. % RDI: 5% calcium, 5% iron, 3% vit A, 2% vit C, 6% folate.

Double-Chocolate Minties

HANDS-ON TIME	TOTAL TIME	MAKES
50 MINUTES	3 HOURS	ABOUT 55 COOKIES

What you need

225 g	semisweet chocolate, chopped
¾ cup	unsalted butter, cubed
1¼ cups	granulated sugar
2	eggs
1¾ cups	all-purpose flour
½ tsp	baking powder
pinch	salt

PEPPERMINT GANACHE:

½ cup	whipping cream (35%)
225 g	70% dark chocolate, finely chopped
2 tsp	peppermint extract

How to make it

In large heatproof bowl over saucepan of hot (not boiling) water, melt chocolate with butter, stirring occasionally until smooth. Remove from heat. Beat in sugar; beat in eggs, 1 at a time. Whisk together flour, baking powder and salt; stir into chocolate mixture. Refrigerate until firm, about 1 hour.

Roll by rounded 1 tsp into balls; place, about 2 inches (5 cm) apart, on parchment paper–lined rimless baking sheets. Bake in 350°F (180°C) oven until firm to the touch and no longer shiny, 8 to 10 minutes.

Let cool on pans on racks for 5 minutes. Transfer to racks; let cool completely. (*Make-ahead: Layer between waxed paper in airtight container and store for up to 5 days.*)

PEPPERMINT GANACHE: In saucepan, bring cream just to boil. Remove from heat; stir in chocolate until smooth. Stir in peppermint extract; let cool to room temperature.

Spoon or pipe about 1 tsp of the ganache onto flat side of half of the cookies; sandwich with remaining cookies, pressing lightly to bring ganache to edge. Refrigerate on baking sheets until ganache is set, about 10 minutes. (*Make-ahead: Refrigerate in airtight container for up to 5 days. Let come to room temperature before serving.*)

NUTRITIONAL INFORMATION, PER COOKIE: about 109 cal, 1 g pro, 7 g total fat (4 g sat. fat), 12 g carb, 1 g fibre, 16 mg chol, 7 mg sodium, 54 mg potassium. % RDI: 1% calcium, 6% iron, 3% vit A, 4% folate.

Chewy

Gluten-Free White Chocolate Pistachio Cookies

HANDS-ON TIME	TOTAL TIME	MAKES
30 MINUTES	1¾ HOURS	32 COOKIES

What you need

3	egg whites
½ cup	granulated sugar
2 cups	ground pistachios
½ cup	gluten-free all-purpose baking flour (such as Bob's Red Mill)
¼ tsp	ground cardamom
pinch	salt
85 g	white chocolate, chopped

How to make it

In large bowl, beat egg whites until soft peaks form; beat in sugar, 2 tbsp at a time, until stiff glossy peaks form. Whisk together 1¾ cups of the pistachios, flour, cardamom and salt; fold into egg whites. Let stand for 5 minutes.

With damp hands, roll by rounded 1 tbsp into balls. Place, 2 inches (5 cm) apart, on parchment paper–lined rimless baking sheets; press into 1½-inch (4 cm) rounds. Bake in 325°F (160°C) oven until firm to the touch and bottoms are golden, 15 to 18 minutes. Let cool on pan on rack.

In heatproof bowl over saucepan of hot (not boiling) water, melt white chocolate. Using piping bag fitted with small plain tip, pipe white chocolate over cooled cookies. Sprinkle with remaining pistachios. Let stand on rack until set. (*Make-ahead: Layer between waxed paper in airtight container and store for up to 5 days.*)

NUTRITIONAL INFORMATION, PER COOKIE: about 61 cal, 2 g pro, 3 g total fat (1 g sat. fat), 7 g carb, 1 g fibre, 0 mg chol, 7 mg sodium. % RDI: 1% calcium, 1% iron, 1% folate.

White Chocolate Cranberry Blondies

HANDS-ON TIME	TOTAL TIME	MAKES
15 MINUTES	55 MINUTES	40 BARS

What you need

1 cup	butter, softened
280 g	white chocolate, chopped
1¼ cups	granulated sugar
4	eggs
2 cups	all-purpose flour
1 cup	dried cranberries
1 tbsp	grated orange zest
1 tbsp	vanilla
½ tsp	salt

How to make it

In saucepan over low heat, melt butter with white chocolate, stirring occasionally until smooth. Let cool for 10 minutes.

Using wooden spoon, stir in sugar; stir in eggs, 1 at a time, stirring well after each. Stir in flour, cranberries, orange zest, vanilla and salt. Spread in parchment paper–lined 13- x 9-inch (3.5 L) cake pan.

Bake in 325°F (160°C) oven until cake tester inserted in centre comes out clean, 30 to 35 minutes.

Cut into bars.

NUTRITIONAL INFORMATION, PER BAR: about 142 cal, 2 g pro, 7 g total fat (4 g sat. fat), 17 g carb, trace fibre, 33 mg chol, 88 mg sodium. % RDI: 2% calcium, 2% iron, 5% vit A, 2% vit C, 5% folate.

Chocolate Caramel Bites

HANDS-ON TIME	TOTAL TIME	MAKES
50 MINUTES	2 HOURS	24 PIECES

What you need

1 cup	pecan halves
pinch	salt
⅔ cup	sweetened condensed milk
½ cup	packed dark brown sugar
½ cup	unsalted butter
2 tbsp	corn syrup
½ tsp	vanilla
55 g	bittersweet chocolate, chopped
2 tbsp	whipping cream (35%)

How to make it

Spread pecans on rimmed baking sheet; sprinkle with salt. Bake in 350°F (180°C) oven until fragrant and golden, about 7 minutes. Let cool.

Remove 24 halves and set aside. Chop remaining pecans; divide evenly among 24 greased mini muffin or tart cups.

In saucepan over medium heat, melt together sweetened condensed milk, brown sugar, butter and corn syrup, stirring until smooth. Simmer over medium-low heat, stirring constantly, until thickened, deep caramel colour and candy thermometer reads 215 to 220°F (102 to 104°C), 25 to 27 minutes. Remove from heat. Immediately stir in vanilla. Spoon 1 tbsp into each cup; tap pans to spread evenly. Let cool in pans on rack.

Meanwhile, in bowl over saucepan of hot (not boiling) water, melt chocolate with cream. Remove from heat; stir until smooth.

Spoon scant ½ tsp chocolate mixture onto centre of each candy. Top each with 1 of the reserved pecan halves. Refrigerate until firm, about 30 minutes. *(Make-ahead: Layer between waxed paper in airtight container and refrigerate for up to 2 weeks.)*

NUTRITIONAL INFORMATION, PER PIECE: about 130 cal, 1 g pro, 9 g total fat (4 g sat. fat), 12 g carb, 1 g fibre, 15 mg chol, 16 mg sodium. % RDI: 3% calcium, 2% iron, 5% vit A, 1% folate.

Oatmeal Chocolate Chip Cookies

HANDS-ON TIME	TOTAL TIME	MAKES
15 MINUTES	1 HOUR	ABOUT 36 COOKIES

What you need

⅔ cup	butter, softened
1 cup	packed brown sugar
1	egg
2 tsp	vanilla
1½ cups	large-flake rolled oats
1 cup	all-purpose flour
½ tsp	each baking powder and baking soda
¼ tsp	salt
1½ cups	semisweet chocolate chips

How to make it

In large bowl, beat butter with brown sugar until fluffy; beat in egg and vanilla. Whisk together oats, flour, baking powder, baking soda and salt; stir into butter mixture until combined. Stir in chocolate chips.

Drop by heaping 1 tbsp, about 2 inches (5 cm) apart, onto parchment paper–lined rimless baking sheets. Bake on top and bottom racks in 375°F (190°C) oven, rotating and switching pans halfway through, until golden, about 12 minutes.

Let cool on pans on racks for 2 minutes. Transfer to racks; let cool completely. *(Make-ahead: Layer between waxed paper in airtight container and store for up to 5 days or freeze for up to 2 weeks.)*

NUTRITIONAL INFORMATION, PER COOKIE: about 119 cal, 1 g pro, 6 g total fat (3 g sat. fat), 16 g carb, 1 g fibre, 16 mg chol, 75 mg sodium. % RDI: 1% calcium, 5% iron, 4% vit A, 4% folate.

Terrine au Chocolat

HANDS-ON TIME		TOTAL TIME		MAKES
25 MINUTES	•	14¼ HOURS	•	12 SERVINGS

What you need

½ cup	granulated sugar
½ cup	strong brewed coffee
1 cup	butter
225 g	bittersweet chocolate, chopped
4	eggs
1 tbsp	all-purpose flour
½ cup	chopped pistachios

How to make it

Line 8- x 4-inch (1.5 L) loaf pan with parchment paper; trim paper even with rim. Set aside.

In heatproof bowl over saucepan of hot (not boiling) water, stir sugar with coffee until dissolved. Add butter and chocolate; melt, stirring occasionally, until smooth. Set aside.

In large bowl, whisk eggs until pale; sift flour over top and whisk in. Fold in chocolate mixture until no streaks remain; pour into prepared pan.

Place pan in larger pan; pour in enough hot water into larger pan to come halfway up sides of loaf pan. Bake in 350°F (180°C) oven until top is set, edges are puffed and centre is still slightly jiggly, about 45 minutes.

Transfer loaf pan to rack; let cool completely. Cover with plastic wrap and refrigerate until firm, about 12 hours. *(Make-ahead: Refrigerate for up to 2 days. Let stand at room temperature for 1 hour before serving.)*

Run knife around sides of pan to loosen paper. Invert serving platter over top; turn over. Remove pan; peel off paper. Sprinkle pistachios over top.

NUTRITIONAL INFORMATION, PER SERVING: about 331 cal, 5 g pro, 26 g total fat (14 g sat. fat), 21 g carb, 2 g fibre, 110 mg chol, 177 mg sodium. % RDI: 3% calcium, 9% iron, 17% vit A, 5% folate.

Candied Orange and Ginger Bark

HANDS-ON TIME	TOTAL TIME	MAKES
45 MINUTES	12½ HOURS	ABOUT 18 SERVINGS

What you need

675 g	bittersweet chocolate, chopped
⅔ cup	shelled pistachios, coarsely chopped
⅓ cup	crystallized ginger, chopped
⅓ cup	dried cranberries

CANDIED ORANGE:

1	orange
2½ cups	granulated sugar

How to make it

CANDIED ORANGE: Cut orange in half from stem to blossom end. Place, cut sides down, on work surface; cut crosswise into ¼-inch (5 mm) thick half-moons.

In saucepan, cover orange slices with cold water and bring to gentle boil; immediately drain, discarding water. With fresh water, repeat boiling and draining twice.

In saucepan, stir 2 cups of the sugar with 2 cups water over medium heat until sugar is dissolved. Add orange slices; reduce heat to low and simmer for 45 minutes.

Using slotted spoon, transfer orange slices to rack over baking sheet; let stand until dry, about 12 hours. *(Make-ahead: Let stand for up to 24 hours.)* Dredge slices in remaining sugar, pressing to coat. Cut each slice into 3 triangles.

In heatproof bowl over saucepan of hot (not boiling) water, melt chocolate, stirring until smooth. Mix together pistachios, ginger and cranberries; stir half into chocolate. Scrape into parchment paper–lined 13- x 9-inch (3.5 L) cake pan, smoothing top. Sprinkle evenly with remaining ginger mixture.

Arrange 18 candied orange pieces on top. Refrigerate until firm, about 45 minutes. Cut into chunks. *(Make-ahead: Refrigerate in airtight container for up to 2 days.)*

NUTRITIONAL INFORMATION, PER SERVING: about 285 cal, 3 g pro, 17 g total fat (9 g sat. fat), 35 g carb, 4 g fibre, 2 mg chol, 6 mg sodium, 376 mg potassium. % RDI: 4% calcium, 25% iron, 1% vit A, 8% vit C, 1% folate.

Ganache-Filled Chocolates

HANDS-ON TIME	TOTAL TIME	MAKES
45 MINUTES	1½ HOURS	24 PIECES

What you need

225 g	70% dark chocolate, grated

GANACHE:

55 g	70% dark chocolate, grated
30 g	milk chocolate, grated
¼ cup	whipping cream (35%)
2 tbsp	liqueur (such as Frangelico, Kahlúa, Tia Maria or amaretto)

TEMPERING CHOCOLATE

The process of heating and cooling chocolate to specific temperatures is called tempering. Tempered chocolate is shiny and has a snappy texture, which makes it excellent for coating truffles and chocolate moulds (as we have done in the recipe on this page). When tempering milk and white chocolates, reduce each of the temperatures listed in this recipe (right) by 2°F (1.7°C).

How to make it

GANACHE: Place dark chocolate and milk chocolate in heatproof bowl. In small saucepan, heat cream until steaming and small bubbles form around edge. Pour over chocolate; stir until melted and smooth. Stir in liqueur. Let cool to room temperature.

Polish chocolate moulds with soft dry cloth or cotton batting; set aside. In heatproof bowl over saucepan of hot (not boiling) water, melt chocolate, stirring often, until smooth and candy thermometer reads 115°F (46°C). Remove bowl from saucepan. Place over bowl of cold water; stir constantly until temperature falls to 80°F (27°C). Replace bowl over hot water or place on heating pad; stir constantly until temperature reaches 88°F (31°C). Hold between 88 and 92°F (31 and 33°C) while moulding.

Place rack over waxed paper– or parchment paper–lined baking sheet; set aside. Spoon tempered chocolate into moulds, filling each to top. Using metal spatula, scrape across top of mould to remove excess; return excess to bowl.

Turn moulds upside down over bowl; tap moulds to remove excess. Let stand upside down on rack for 30 seconds, allowing excess to drip out, leaving thin coating on moulds. Scrape to level top of moulds. Refrigerate for 5 minutes.

Using pastry bag fitted with ¼-inch (5 mm) plain tip, pipe ganache into each mould until ⅛ inch (3 mm) from top. Tap mould gently. Refrigerate for 10 minutes.

If necessary, reheat remaining tempered chocolate to between 88 and 92°F (31 and 33°C). Pour over ganache in moulds. Using metal spatula, scrape across top of mould to remove excess; return excess to bowl. Refrigerate until chocolate is set and has shrunk away from sides of moulds, about 20 minutes. Unmould onto tray. *(Make-ahead: Store in airtight container at room temperature for up to 2 weeks.)*

NUTRITIONAL INFORMATION, PER PIECE: about 90 cal, 1 g pro, 6 g total fat (4 g sat. fat), 7 g carb, 1 g fibre, 4 mg chol, 6 mg sodium, 86 mg potassium. % RDI: 1% calcium, 10% iron, 1% vit A.

Earl Grey Chocolate Truffles

HANDS-ON TIME	TOTAL TIME	MAKES
1¼ HOURS	5¾ HOURS	36 TRUFFLES

What you need

⅔ cup	whipping cream (35%)
2 tsp	loose leaf Earl Grey tea
1	strip orange zest
¼ cup	unsalted butter, cubed
225 g	milk chocolate, finely chopped

COATING:

170 g	each milk chocolate and bittersweet chocolate, finely chopped

PIPING:

30 g	white chocolate, milk chocolate or bittersweet chocolate, finely chopped

How to make it

In saucepan, heat cream until bubbles form around edge; remove from heat. Stir in tea and orange zest; cover and let steep for 1 hour. Strain though cheesecloth-lined sieve into clean saucepan. Add butter; heat until melted and bubbles form around edge.

Place chocolate in heatproof bowl. Pour in cream mixture, whisking until chocolate is melted and smooth. Cover and refrigerate until firm, about 1 hour.

Using melon baller or teaspoon, drop by heaping 1 tsp onto waxed paper–lined rimmed baking sheets to make 36 pieces. Gently roll each ball between fingertips to round off. Freeze until hard, about 1 hour. Reroll to smooth edges; freeze. (*Make-ahead: Cover and freeze for up to 24 hours.*)

COATING: In heatproof bowl over saucepan of hot (not boiling) water, melt milk chocolate with bittersweet chocolate, stirring, until no large pieces remain and candy thermometer reads 113°F (45°C). Remove bowl from saucepan. Place over bowl of cold water; stir constantly until temperature falls to 78°F (26°C). Replace bowl over hot water or place on heating pad; stir constantly until temperature reaches 86°F (30°C); hold between 86 and 90°F (30 and 32°C) while using.

Using candy-dipping fork or 2 forks, dip each truffle centre into chocolate, tapping fork on edge of bowl to remove excess. Place on waxed paper–lined rimmed baking sheet. Refrigerate until coating is hardened, about 2 hours.

PIPING: In heatproof bowl over saucepan of hot (not boiling) water, melt chocolate, stirring until smooth. Spoon into piping bag fitted with writing tip. Pipe swirl or monogram onto top of each truffle. Refrigerate until hardened, about 30 minutes. (*Make-ahead: Layer between waxed paper in airtight container and refrigerate for up to 1 week.*) Place in paper candy cups.

NUTRITIONAL INFORMATION, PER TRUFFLE: about 105 cal, 1 g pro, 8 g total fat (5 g sat. fat), 9 g carb, 1 g fibre, 11 mg chol, 10 mg sodium. % RDI: 2% calcium, 2% iron, 3% vit A.

Dark Chocolate Truffles

HANDS-ON TIME	TOTAL TIME	MAKES
1½ HOURS	5 HOURS	ABOUT 32 TRUFFLES

What you need

225 g	semisweet chocolate or bittersweet chocolate, finely chopped
⅔ cup	whipping cream (35%)
¼ cup	butter, cubed
1 tbsp	vanilla

COATING:

225 g	semisweet chocolate or bittersweet chocolate, finely chopped

How to make it

Place chocolate in heatproof bowl. In saucepan, heat cream with butter just until butter is melted and bubbles form around edge. Pour over chocolate; whisk until smooth. Whisk in vanilla. Cover and refrigerate until firm, about 2 hours.

Using melon baller or teaspoon, drop by rounded 1 tsp onto waxed paper–lined rimmed baking sheets. Gently roll each ball between fingertips to round off. Freeze until hard, about 1 hour. *(Make-ahead: Cover and freeze for up to 24 hours.)*

COATING: In heatproof bowl over saucepan of hot (not boiling) water, melt half of the chocolate at a time, stirring often. Remove from heat and let cool slightly.

Working with 1 pan of truffles at a time and using 2 forks, dip each into chocolate, tapping forks on edge of bowl to remove excess. Return to waxed paper–lined baking sheet. Refrigerate until coating is hardened, about 2 hours. *(Make-ahead: Layer between waxed paper in airtight container and refrigerate for up to 1 week or freeze for up to 3 months.)*

Place in candy cups, if desired.

VARIATION

Cinnamon Pistachio Truffles

Add ½ tsp cinnamon along with vanilla. After dipping truffles in coating, roll in 1½ cups finely chopped natural pistachios.

Hazelnut Truffles

Reduce whipping cream to ½ cup; replace vanilla with 3 tbsp hazelnut liqueur (such as Frangelico). After dipping truffles in coating, roll in 1½ cups finely chopped toasted hazelnuts.

NUTRITIONAL INFORMATION, PER TRUFFLE: about 93 cal, 1 g pro, 7 g total fat (4 g sat. fat), 9 g carb, 1 g fibre, 10 mg chol, 13 mg sodium, 53 mg potassium. % RDI: 1% calcium, 3% iron, 3% vit A.

**Cinnamon
Pistachio Truffles**
opposite (variation)

**Dark Chocolate
Truffles**
opposite

Brazilian Brigadeiros

HANDS-ON TIME	TOTAL TIME	MAKES
30 MINUTES	50 MINUTES	36 PIECES

What you need

3 tbsp	cocoa powder, sifted
1	can (300 mL) sweetened condensed milk
1 tbsp	unsalted butter
½ cup	chocolate shot (see tip, below)

How to make it

In bowl, stir cocoa powder with ¼ cup of the sweetened condensed milk until smooth. Stir in remaining sweetened condensed milk.

In small saucepan, melt butter over medium heat. Using heatproof spatula, stir in milk mixture; cook, stirring constantly and scraping bottom of pan to prevent scorching, until thickened, glossy and mixture holds wide trail after spatula is pulled through centre, 12 to 14 minutes. Immediately scrape into buttered shallow dish. Let cool enough to handle, about 20 minutes.

Place chocolate shot in small shallow bowl. With well-buttered hands, roll milk mixture by 1 tsp into balls; immediately roll each in chocolate shot. (*Make-ahead: Layer between waxed paper in airtight container and store for up to 24 hours.*)

Nestle into paper candy cups, if desired.

TIP FROM THE TEST KITCHEN

Chocolate shot are also known by the names chocolate sprinkles and Chocolate Décors. These thin, dark brown sprinkles are about ¼ inch (5 mm) long. They're easy to find in bulk food stores and the baking aisle of the supermarket.

NUTRITIONAL INFORMATION, PER PIECE: about 46 cal, 1 g pro, 1 g total fat (1 g sat. fat), 8 g carb, trace fibre, 5 mg chol, 14 mg sodium, 52 mg potassium. % RDI: 3% calcium, 1% iron, 1% vit A.

Coconut Rum Truffles

HANDS-ON TIME	TOTAL TIME	MAKES
40 MINUTES	6¾ HOURS	36 TRUFFLES

What you need

115 g	each milk chocolate and bittersweet chocolate, finely chopped
⅔ cup	whipping cream (35%)
¼ cup	unsalted butter, cubed
2 tbsp	amber rum

COATING:

1½ cups	sweetened shredded coconut
225 g	70% bittersweet chocolate, finely chopped

How to make it

Place milk chocolate and bittersweet chocolate in heatproof bowl. In saucepan, heat cream with butter until butter is melted and bubbles form around edge; pour over chocolate, whisking until smooth. Whisk in rum. Cover and refrigerate until firm, about 3 hours.

Using melon baller or teaspoon, drop by heaping 1 tsp onto 2 waxed paper–lined rimmed baking sheets to make 36 pieces. Gently roll each ball between fingertips to round off. Refrigerate until hard, about 1 hour. Reroll to smooth edges; refrigerate. (*Make-ahead: Refrigerate for up to 24 hours.*)

COATING: Meanwhile, on baking sheet, toast coconut in 300°F (150°C) oven, stirring often, until golden and fragrant, 6 to 7 minutes. Transfer to shallow dish; let cool. In heatproof bowl over saucepan of hot (not boiling) water, melt chocolate, stirring until smooth.

Using candy-dipping fork or 2 forks, dip each truffle centre into chocolate, tapping fork on edge of bowl to remove excess. Roll in coconut.

Return to waxed paper–lined rimmed baking sheet. Refrigerate until coating is hardened, about 2 hours. (*Make-ahead: Layer between waxed paper in airtight container and refrigerate for up to 2 weeks or freeze for up to 1 month.*)

NUTRITIONAL INFORMATION, PER TRUFFLE: about 97 cal, 1 g pro, 8 g total fat (5 g sat. fat), 7 g carb, 1 g fibre, 10 mg chol, 15 mg sodium. % RDI: 1% calcium, 6% iron, 3% vit A.

Chocolate Cherry Cups

HANDS-ON TIME		TOTAL TIME		MAKES
45 MINUTES		2½ HOURS		30 PIECES

What you need

280 g	70% dark chocolate, chopped
170 g	milk chocolate, chopped
1	pkg (200 g) marzipan
½ cup	glacé cherries

GARNISH:

10	glacé cherries, cut in thirds

How to make it

In heatproof bowl over saucepan of hot (not boiling) water, melt together half each of the dark chocolate and milk chocolate, stirring until smooth. Pour about 1 tsp into each of thirty 1¾-inch (4.5 cm) wide candy cups. Refrigerate until firm, about 30 minutes.

Meanwhile, in food processor, pulse marzipan with cherries until smooth paste forms. Roll by fully rounded 1 tsp into balls. Gently press balls into candy cups, flattening tops almost but not all the way to edge.

In heatproof bowl over saucepan of hot (not boiling) water, melt together remaining dark and milk chocolates; pour 1 tsp over each filling to cover, smoothing top. Refrigerate for 10 minutes.

GARNISH: Top each chocolate with 1 cherry piece. Refrigerate until firm, about 1 hour. (*Make-ahead: Layer between waxed paper in airtight container and refrigerate for up to 1 week.*)

TIP FROM THE TEST KITCHEN
Almond paste and marzipan are both made from almonds and sugar, but they aren't interchangeable in recipes. Marzipan contains more sugar and is designed for moulding into shapes and use in confections like these cherry cups.

NUTRITIONAL INFORMATION, PER PIECE: about 131 cal, 2 g pro, 8 g total fat (4 g sat. fat), 15 g carb, 2 g fibre, 2 mg chol, 8 mg sodium, 123 mg potassium. % RDI: 2% calcium, 9% iron, 1% folate.

Triple-Nut Chocolate Fudge

HANDS-ON TIME	TOTAL TIME	MAKES
15 MINUTES	3¼ HOURS	36 PIECES

What you need

450 g	semisweet chocolate or 70% dark chocolate, chopped
1	can (300 mL) sweetened condensed milk
1 tsp	vanilla
½ cup	chopped roasted cashews
½ cup	chopped pecans
½ cup	chopped walnuts

How to make it

In bowl over saucepan of hot (not boiling) water, melt chocolate with sweetened condensed milk, stirring frequently, until smooth, about 5 minutes. Stir in vanilla. Stir in cashews, pecans and walnuts.

Pour into parchment paper–lined 9-inch (2.5 L) square cake pan; smooth top. Refrigerate until firm, about 3 hours.

Using paper as handles, transfer fudge to cutting board; peel off paper. Cut into 36 pieces. (*Make-ahead: Layer between waxed paper in airtight container and refrigerate for up to 2 weeks.*)

VARIATION

S'mores Fudge

Substitute 1½ cups mini marshmallows and 1 cup coarsely broken graham crackers for the chopped nuts.

TIP FROM THE TEST KITCHEN
To cut fudge into neat squares, dip a sharp chef's knife into hot water and wipe it dry before making each slice.

NUTRITIONAL INFORMATION, PER PIECE: about 127 cal, 2 g pro, 8 g total fat (3 g sat. fat), 15 g carb, 1 g fibre, 4 mg chol, 15 mg sodium, 111 mg potassium. % RDI: 3% calcium, 4% iron, 1% vit A, 2% folate.

Easy Chocolate Walnut Fudge

HANDS-ON TIME	TOTAL TIME	MAKES
25 MINUTES	2½ HOURS	64 PIECES

What you need

1 cup	coarsely chopped walnuts
280 g	bittersweet chocolate or semisweet chocolate, chopped
1	can (300 mL) sweetened condensed milk
1 tsp	vanilla
¼ tsp	baking soda
pinch	salt

How to make it

On baking sheet, toast walnuts in 350°F (180°C) oven until fragrant, about 6 minutes. Let cool.

In heatproof bowl over saucepan of hot (not boiling) water, melt bittersweet chocolate, stirring until smooth. Remove from heat. Stir in condensed milk, vanilla, baking soda and salt until smooth. Stir in walnuts.

Immediately spread in parchment paper–lined 8-inch (2 L) square cake pan. Refrigerate until set, about 2 hours.

Using paper as handles, transfer fudge to cutting board. Using hot dry knife, cut into 64 pieces.

TIP FROM THE TEST KITCHEN

Nuts aren't cheap, so you don't want to waste them. Buy them from a store with high turnover so you're getting the freshest ones. To prevent their natural oils from going rancid, freeze nuts in a tightly sealed plastic freezer bag. You don't need to thaw them; just take out the amount you need a couple of minutes ahead and they'll be fresh and ready to use.

NUTRITIONAL INFORMATION, PER PIECE: about 57 cal, 1 g pro, 3 g total fat (1 g sat. fat), 6 g carb, 1 g fibre, 2 mg chol, 13 mg sodium, 31 mg potassium. % RDI: 2% calcium, 2% iron, 1% vit A, 1% folate.

Crispy Coffee Truffle Slice

HANDS-ON TIME	TOTAL TIME	MAKES
35 MINUTES	5½ HOURS	36 PIECES

What you need

225 g	white chocolate, finely chopped
¼ cup	whipping cream (35%)
2 tbsp	unsalted butter

MILK CHOCOLATE COFFEE GANACHE:

225 g	milk chocolate, finely chopped
½ cup	whipping cream (35%)
2 tbsp	unsalted butter
1 tbsp	instant coffee granules
1 tsp	vanilla

CRISPY DARK CHOCOLATE GANACHE:

225 g	70% dark chocolate, finely chopped
⅓ cup	whipping cream (35%)
2 tbsp	unsalted butter
1 cup	rice crisp cereal

How to make it

In heatproof bowl over saucepan of hot (not boiling) water, melt together white chocolate, cream and butter, stirring occasionally until smooth. Pour into parchment paper–lined 8-inch (2 L) square cake pan; using small offset spatula, smooth to edge. Refrigerate until firm, about 1½ hours.

MILK CHOCOLATE COFFEE GANACHE: In heatproof bowl over saucepan of hot (not boiling) water, melt milk chocolate, cream, butter, coffee granules and vanilla, stirring occasionally, until melted and smooth.

Pour over white chocolate ganache; using small offset spatula, smooth to edge. Refrigerate until firm, about 1½ hours.

CRISPY DARK CHOCOLATE GANACHE: In heatproof bowl over saucepan of hot (not boiling) water, melt together dark chocolate, cream and butter, stirring often until smooth. Remove from heat; stir in cereal.

Pour over milk chocolate coffee ganache; using small offset spatula, smooth to edge. Refrigerate until firm, about 2 hours.

Using paper as handles, invert onto cutting board; peel off paper. Wiping thin sharp knife with damp cloth between slices, trim edges to even; cut into 36 pieces. (*Make-ahead: Layer between waxed paper in airtight container and refrigerate for up to 1 week.*) Place in candy cups if desired.

NUTRITIONAL INFORMATION, PER PIECE: about 146 cal, 2 g pro, 11 g total fat (7 g sat. fat), 11 g carb, 1 g fibre, 16 mg chol, 19 mg sodium, 100 mg potassium. % RDI: 3% calcium, 6% iron, 4% vit A.

Crispy Coffee
Truffle Slice
opposite

Triple-Nut
Chocolate Fudge
page 90

Classic Nanaimo Bars

HANDS-ON TIME	TOTAL TIME	MAKES
20 MINUTES	2¾ HOURS	25 BARS

What you need

1 cup	graham cracker crumbs
½ cup	sweetened shredded coconut
⅓ cup	finely chopped walnuts
¼ cup	cocoa powder
¼ cup	granulated sugar
⅓ cup	butter, melted
1	egg, lightly beaten

FILLING:

¼ cup	butter, softened
2 tbsp	custard powder
½ tsp	vanilla
2 cups	icing sugar
2 tbsp	milk (approx)

TOPPING:

115 g	semisweet chocolate, chopped
1 tbsp	butter

How to make it

In bowl, stir together graham cracker crumbs, coconut, walnuts, cocoa powder and sugar. Drizzle with butter and egg; stir until moistened.

Press into parchment paper–lined 9-inch (2.5 L) square cake pan. Bake in 350°F (180°C) oven until firm, about 10 minutes. Let cool in pan on rack.

FILLING: In bowl, beat together butter, custard powder and vanilla. Beat in icing sugar alternately with milk, making 3 additions of sugar and 2 of milk and adding up to 1 tsp more milk if too thick to spread. Spread over cooled base. Refrigerate until firm, about 1 hour.

TOPPING: In heatproof bowl over saucepan of hot (not boiling) water, melt chocolate with butter, stirring until smooth; spread over filling. Refrigerate until chocolate is almost set, about 30 minutes.

With tip of sharp knife, score into 25 bars; refrigerate until chocolate is completely set, about 30 minutes. *(Make-ahead: Remove from pan. Wrap in plastic wrap and refrigerate for up to 4 days or overwrap in foil and freeze for up to 2 weeks.)*

Cut into bars.

NUTRITIONAL INFORMATION, PER BAR: about 150 cal, 1 g pro, 9 g total fat (5 g sat. fat), 19 g carb, 1 g fibre, 20 mg chol, 65 mg sodium, 62 mg potassium. % RDI: 1% calcium, 4% iron, 4% vit A, 2% folate.

Reverse Nanaimo Bars

HANDS-ON TIME	TOTAL TIME	MAKES
20 MINUTES	2¾ HOURS	25 BARS

What you need

1½ cups	graham cracker crumbs
½ cup	sweetened shredded coconut
¼ cup	finely chopped almonds
30 g	white chocolate, chopped
¼ cup	butter, melted
1	egg, lightly beaten

FILLING:

⅓ cup	butter
⅔ cup	cocoa powder
1⅓ cups	icing sugar
3 tbsp	milk
2 tbsp	custard powder
1 tsp	vanilla

TOPPING:

225 g	white chocolate, coarsely chopped
½ tsp	butter
10 g	dark chocolate, shaved

How to make it

In bowl, stir together graham cracker crumbs, coconut, almonds and chocolate. Drizzle with butter and egg; stir until moistened.

Press into parchment paper–lined 9-inch (2.5 L) square cake pan. Bake in 350°F (180°C) oven until firm, about 10 minutes. Let cool in pan on rack.

FILLING: In heavy saucepan, melt butter over low heat; stir in cocoa powder until smooth. Pour into bowl; beat in icing sugar, milk, custard powder and vanilla until smooth. Spread over cooled base; refrigerate until firm, about 1 hour.

TOPPING: In heatproof bowl over saucepan of hot (not boiling) water, melt white chocolate with butter, stirring until smooth; spread over filling. Refrigerate until chocolate is almost set, about 30 minutes.

With tip of sharp knife, score into bars; sprinkle with shaved chocolate. Refrigerate until chocolate is completely set, about 30 minutes. (*Make-ahead: Remove from pan. Wrap in plastic wrap and refrigerate for up to 4 days or overwrap in foil and freeze for up to 2 weeks.*)

Cut into bars.

NUTRITIONAL INFORMATION, PER BAR: about 164 cal, 2 g pro, 10 g total fat (6 g sat. fat), 18 g carb, 1 g fibre, 20 mg chol, 82 mg sodium, 116 mg potassium. % RDI: 3% calcium, 5% iron, 4% vit A, 3% folate.

Chocolate Silk Tartlet Trio

HANDS-ON TIME	TOTAL TIME	MAKES
1 HOUR	4 HOURS	24 TARTLETS

What you need

1 cup	all-purpose flour
½ cup	icing sugar
⅓ cup	cold butter, cubed
1	egg yolk

WHITE CHOCOLATE SILK:

45 g	white chocolate, finely chopped
¾ tsp	bourbon or rum
3 tbsp	whipping cream (35%)
2 tbsp	toasted chopped pecans

MILK CHOCOLATE MOCHA SILK:

¾ tsp	instant coffee granules
3 tbsp	whipping cream (35%)
55 g	milk chocolate, finely chopped
15 g	semisweet chocolate, shaved

DARK CHOCOLATE SILK:

45 g	semisweet chocolate or bittersweet chocolate, finely chopped
1 tsp	butter
¼ cup	whipping cream (35%)
8	raspberries

How to make it

In bowl, whisk flour with sugar; using pastry blender, cut in butter until in fine crumbs. Whisk egg yolk with 1 tbsp water; stir into flour mixture just until dough begins to clump. On floured surface, knead dough a few times to form ball; press into disc. Cover and refrigerate until firm, 1 hour.

Between waxed paper, roll out dough to scant ⅛-inch (3 mm) thickness. Using 2-inch (5 cm) round cutter, cut out 24 rounds. Press into 2¾ - x 1¼-inch (7 x 3 cm) tartlet or muffin cups; freeze for 1 hour.

Prick bottoms all over with tip of knife. Bake in 350°F (180°C) oven, gently pressing with back of spoon if puffing, until golden, about 20 minutes. Let cool in pan on rack. (*Make-ahead: Store in airtight container for up to 3 days or freeze for up to 2 weeks.*)

WHITE CHOCOLATE SILK: In heatproof bowl over saucepan of hot (not boiling) water, heat white chocolate with bourbon until three-quarters is melted. Remove from heat; stir until melted. Stir in cream until smooth. Place over bowl of ice water; beat just until thickness of icing (do not overbeat). Scatter some of the pecans in 8 of the tart shells. Using piping bag fitted with medium star tip, pipe silk into shells. Garnish with remaining pecans.

MILK CHOCOLATE MOCHA SILK: Dissolve coffee granules in ¼ tsp water; add cream. Melt milk and semisweet chocolates as directed for white chocolate silk (above); stir in cream mixture until smooth. Beat and pipe as directed. Garnish with shaved chocolate.

DARK CHOCOLATE SILK: Melt semisweet chocolate with butter as directed for white chocolate silk (above); stir in cream until smooth. Beat and pipe as directed. Garnish with raspberries. (*Make-ahead: Refrigerate tartlets in airtight container for up to 24 hours.*)

NUTRITIONAL INFORMATION, PER WHITE CHOCOLATE SILK TARTLET: about 189 cal, 2 g pro, 12 g total fat (6 g sat. fat), 19 g carb, 1 g fibre, 44 mg chol, 51 mg sodium. % RDI: 2% calcium, 5% iron, 8% vit A, 13% folate.

NUTRITIONAL INFORMATION, PER MILK CHOCOLATE MOCHA SILK TARTLET: about 191 cal, 2 g pro, 11 g total fat (7 g sat. fat), 21 g carb, 1 g fibre, 46 mg chol, 54 mg sodium. % RDI: 2% calcium, 6% iron, 9% vit A, 13% folate.

NUTRITIONAL INFORMATION, PER DARK CHOCOLATE SILK TARTLET: about 186 cal, 2 g pro, 11 g total fat (7 g sat. fat), 20 g carb, 1 g fibre, 48 mg chol, 51 mg sodium. % RDI: 1% calcium, 6% iron, 9% vit A, 2% vit C, 14% folate.

Chocolate Almond Tartlets

HANDS-ON TIME	TOTAL TIME	MAKES
1 HOUR	3½ HOURS	24 TARTS

What you need

340 g	bittersweet chocolate, chopped
⅔ cup	whipping cream (35%)
2 tbsp	almond liqueur (such as amaretto)
⅓ cup	almonds, toasted

CHOCOLATE PASTRY:

⅓ cup	butter, softened
¼ cup	granulated sugar
1	egg yolk
½ tsp	vanilla
¾ cup	all-purpose flour (approx)
3 tbsp	cocoa powder
pinch	salt

How to make it

CHOCOLATE PASTRY: In large bowl, beat butter with sugar until fluffy; beat in egg yolk and vanilla. Into separate bowl, sift together flour, cocoa powder and salt; sift again. Stir into butter mixture in 2 additions. Gather into ball; press into disc. Wrap in plastic wrap; refrigerate until chilled, about 1 hour.

On lightly floured surface, roll out pastry to ⅛-inch (3 mm) thickness. Using 2½-inch (6 cm) round cutter, cut out 24 circles; gently press into 1½- x ¾-inch (4 x 2 cm) fluted tart pans. Place on baking sheet; refrigerate until firm, about 20 minutes. Prick bottoms of each tart shell twice with fork. Bake in 375°F (190°C) oven until firm and no longer shiny, about 15 minutes. Let cool on pan on rack.

Meanwhile, place half of the chocolate in heatproof bowl. In saucepan, bring cream just to boil; pour over chocolate, whisking until smooth. Whisk in liqueur. Cover and refrigerate until mixture is thick enough to mound on spoon, about 1 hour.

Chop almonds to about size of lemon seeds; remove 3 tbsp and set aside for garnish. Sprinkle ½ tsp of the remaining almonds into each tart shell. Set aside.

Beat chocolate mixture until thick and fluffy. Spoon mousse by rounded 1 tbsp into shells, rounding and smoothing tops with small palette knife. Refrigerate until firm, about 15 minutes.

Meanwhile, in separate heatproof bowl over saucepan of hot (not boiling) water, melt remaining chocolate. Let cool to room temperature. Spoon enough over mousse to cover just to edge of crust. Sprinkle reserved almonds around edge. Refrigerate until set, about 5 minutes. *(Make-ahead: Refrigerate in single layer in shallow airtight container for up to 2 days.)*

NUTRITIONAL INFORMATION, PER TART: about 167 cal, 3 g pro, 15 g total fat (8 g sat. fat), 11 g carb, 3 g fibre, 25 mg chol, 32 mg sodium. % RDI: 2% calcium, 9% iron, 5% vit A, 4% folate.

Chocolate Fruit and Nut Tart

HANDS-ON TIME
35 MINUTES

TOTAL TIME
3 HOURS

MAKES
12 SERVINGS

What you need

⅓ cup	dried currants
⅓ cup	chopped pitted prunes
¼ cup	brandy
⅓ cup	each walnut halves and natural almonds
⅓ cup	unsalted butter, softened
½ cup	granulated sugar
2	eggs
3 tbsp	all-purpose flour
115 g	bittersweet chocolate, finely chopped

SWEET PASTRY:

1¼ cups	all-purpose flour
¾ cup	icing sugar
1 tsp	grated orange zest
pinch	salt
½ cup	unsalted butter, softened
2	egg yolks

How to make it

In small bowl, stir together currants, prunes and brandy; cover and let stand for 1 hour.

On baking sheet, toast walnuts and almonds in 350°F (180°C) oven until fragrant, 8 to 10 minutes. Let cool; coarsely chop.

SWEET PASTRY: Meanwhile, in food processor, pulse together flour, sugar, orange zest and salt. Pulse in butter until mixture resembles coarse meal. Pulse in egg yolks until pastry clumps together. Gather into ball; press into disc. Wrap in plastic wrap; refrigerate until firm, about 1 hour. (*Make-ahead: Refrigerate for up to 24 hours.*)

On lightly floured surface, roll out pastry into 12-inch (30 cm) circle; place in 9-inch (23 cm) round tart pan with removable bottom, pressing to inside edge and leaving overhang. Using rolling pin, roll across rim to trim off overhang.

With fork, prick bottom of pastry all over; refrigerate for 20 minutes. Line with foil; fill with pie weights or dried beans. Bake on bottom rack in 400°F (200°C) oven for 20 minutes. Remove weights and foil; bake until centre is golden, 3 to 7 minutes.

In bowl, beat butter until fluffy; gradually beat in sugar. Beat in eggs, 1 at a time. Stir in flour, chocolate, brandy-soaked fruit and nuts; pour into baked crust.

Bake in 350°F (180°C) oven until centre jiggles slightly and edge is browned, 20 to 25 minutes. Let cool in pan on rack. (*Make-ahead: Let stand at room temperature for up to 8 hours.*)

NUTRITIONAL INFORMATION, PER SERVING: about 345 cal, 5 g pro, 21 g total fat (10 g sat. fat), 36 g carb, 3 g fibre, 89 mg chol, 15 mg sodium, 140 mg potassium. % RDI: 3% calcium, 11% iron, 13% vit A, 17% folate.

Cranberry White Chocolate Tarts

HANDS-ON TIME	TOTAL TIME	MAKES
45 MINUTES	4 HOURS	24 TARTS

What you need

¼ cup	unsweetened dried cranberries
2 tbsp	orange liqueur (such as Grand Marnier) or orange juice
2 tbsp	whipping cream (35%)
55 g	white chocolate, finely chopped
2 tsp	butter, softened

SINGLE-CRUST ALL-PURPOSE PASTRY:

1½ cups	all-purpose flour
½ tsp	salt
¼ cup	each cold butter and lard, cubed
1	egg yolk
1 tsp	vinegar or lemon juice
	ice water

How to make it

SINGLE-CRUST ALL-PURPOSE PASTRY: In bowl, whisk flour with salt. Using pastry blender, cut in butter and lard until mixture is in fine crumbs with a few larger pieces. In liquid measure, whisk egg yolk with vinegar; add enough ice water to make ⅓ cup. Drizzle over dry ingredients, stirring briskly with fork until ragged dough forms. Press into disc; wrap in plastic wrap and refrigerate until chilled, about 30 minutes. *(Make-ahead: Refrigerate for up to 3 days.)*

On lightly floured surface, roll out pastry to ⅛-inch (3 mm) thickness. Using 2½-inch (6 cm) round cutter, cut out 24 circles, rerolling and cutting scraps. Fit into ¾-inch (2 cm) deep mini tart or mini muffin tins. Prick all over with fork; cover and freeze until firm. Bake in 350°F (180°C) oven until golden, about 25 minutes. Let cool in pans on rack.

Meanwhile, in saucepan, cover and heat cranberries with liqueur over medium-low heat until steaming. Remove from heat; let stand until softened. Finely chop.

In small saucepan, bring cream just to boil. Remove from heat; whisk in white chocolate and butter until melted.

Divide cranberries among tart shells; top with chocolate mixture. Refrigerate until set, about 2 hours. *(Make-ahead: Cover and refrigerate for up to 2 days.)*

TIP FROM THE TEST KITCHEN
For this recipe, look for unsweetened dried cranberries at your local health food or bulk food store.

NUTRITIONAL INFORMATION, PER TART: about 84 cal, 1 g pro, 5 g total fat (3 g sat. fat), 8 g carb, trace fibre, 17 mg chol, 63 mg sodium. % RDI: 1% calcium, 2% iron, 3% vit A, 7% folate.

Triple-Berry Chocolate Tart

HANDS-ON TIME	TOTAL TIME	MAKES
30 MINUTES	3¾ HOURS	8 SERVINGS

What you need

170 g	each blackberries, raspberries and blueberries
¼ cup	seedless raspberry jam

CHOCOLATE CRUST:

½ cup	butter, softened
⅓ cup	granulated sugar
1	egg yolk
½ tsp	vanilla
1 cup	all-purpose flour
⅓ cup	cocoa powder
¼ tsp	baking powder
pinch	salt

GANACHE:

225 g	dark chocolate, chopped
1½ cups	whipping cream (35%)

How to make it

CHOCOLATE CRUST: In bowl, beat butter with sugar until fluffy; beat in egg yolk and vanilla. Whisk together flour, cocoa powder, baking powder and salt; stir into butter mixture. Press onto bottom and up side of greased 9-inch (23 cm) round tart pan with removable bottom. Refrigerate for 30 minutes. Bake on baking sheet in 350°F (180°C) oven until surface appears dry, about 30 minutes. Let cool in pan on rack.

GANACHE: Place chocolate in heatproof bowl. In small saucepan, bring cream just to boil; pour over chocolate. Let stand for 2 minutes; whisk until chocolate is melted and smooth. Pour into prepared crust; refrigerate for 2 hours. *(Make-ahead: Cover loosely and refrigerate for up to 24 hours.)*

Arrange blackberries around edge of tart; place 1 in centre. Arrange raspberries inside blackberries; place 5 around centre blackberry. Fill empty space with blueberries.

In small microwaveable dish, microwave raspberry jam with 1 tbsp water on high until liquid, about 40 seconds; brush over berries. Let stand at room temperature for 45 minutes before serving.

TIP FROM THE TEST KITCHEN
You can use any seedless jam to glaze the fruit on this tart. Apricot, peach and strawberry are other delicious options.

NUTRITIONAL INFORMATION, PER SERVING: about 579 cal, 6 g pro, 40 g total fat (24 g sat. fat), 54 g carb, 7 g fibre, 115 mg chol, 116 mg sodium, 408 mg potassium.% RDI: 7% calcium, 25% iron, 26% vit A, 15% vit C, 21% folate.

Chocolate Mousse Pie

HANDS-ON TIME
45 MINUTES

TOTAL TIME
3½ HOURS

MAKES
16 SERVINGS

What you need

225 g	semisweet chocolate, finely chopped
1⅔ cups	whipping cream (35%)
¼ cup	hazelnut liqueur (such as Frangelico)

CHOCOLATE PASTRY:

½ cup	butter, softened
¼ cup	granulated sugar
1	egg yolk
½ tsp	vanilla
1 cup	all-purpose flour
3 tbsp	cocoa powder
pinch	each baking powder and salt

GARNISH:

¾ cup	whipping cream (35%)
1 tbsp	sliced hazelnuts, toasted

How to make it

CHOCOLATE PASTRY: In bowl, beat butter with sugar until light; beat in egg yolk and vanilla. Sift together flour, cocoa powder, baking powder and salt; stir into butter mixture in 2 additions to make soft dough. With wet or floured hands, press onto bottom and up side of 9-inch (23 cm) round tart pan with removable bottom; prick all over with fork. Freeze until firm, about 20 minutes.

Line pie shell with greased foil, greased side down; fill with pie weights or dried beans. Bake on bottom rack in 400°F (200°C) oven for 15 minutes. Remove weights and foil. Bake until firm and edges are darkened, about 8 minutes. Let cool in pan on rack.

Meanwhile, place chocolate in heatproof bowl. In small saucepan, bring ⅔ cup of the cream just to boil; pour over chocolate, whisking until smooth. Whisk in hazelnut liqueur. Let stand, stirring occasionally, until slightly thickened and cooled, 15 to 20 minutes.

Whip remaining cream; fold one-third into chocolate mixture. Fold in remaining whipped cream. Scrape into cooled crust, swirling top. Refrigerate until set, about 2 hours. *(Make-ahead: Cover loosely and refrigerate for up to 24 hours.)*

GARNISH: Whip cream; pipe or spoon around edge of tart. Sprinkle hazelnuts over cream.

TIP FROM THE TEST KITCHEN
You can substitute almond liqueur (such as amaretto) and almonds for the hazelnut liqueur and nuts.

NUTRITIONAL INFORMATION, PER SERVING: about 305 cal, 3 g pro, 23 g total fat (14 g sat. fat), 22 g carb, 2 g fibre, 75 mg chol, 55 mg sodium. % RDI: 3% calcium, 7% iron, 19% vit A, 11% folate.

White Chocolate Hazelnut Pie

HANDS-ON TIME	•	TOTAL TIME	•	MAKES
45 MINUTES		6¼ HOURS		8 SERVINGS

What you need

1¼ cups	all-purpose flour
1 tbsp	icing sugar
¼ tsp	salt
⅓ cup	cold butter, cubed
⅓ cup	whipping cream (35%)
⅓ cup	chocolate hazelnut spread (such as Nutella)

FILLING:

½ cup	hazelnuts
2	eggs
⅓ cup	granulated sugar
2 tbsp	hazelnut liqueur (or 1 tsp vanilla)
170 g	white chocolate, finely chopped
1 cup	whipping cream (35%)

How to make it

In bowl, whisk together flour, sugar and salt. Using pastry blender or 2 knives, cut in butter until in fine crumbs with a few larger pieces. Drizzle in cream, tossing with fork until dough clumps together. Press onto bottom and up side of 9-inch (23 cm) round tart pan with removable bottom. Refrigerate for 30 minutes.

Prick bottom of pastry all over with fork; bake in 375°F (190°C) oven until golden, about 25 minutes. Let cool in pan on rack. Spread chocolate-hazelnut spread over pie shell. Cover and refrigerate for 1 hour.

FILLING: On baking sheet, toast hazelnuts in 350°F (180°C) oven until fragrant and skins crack, about 10 minutes. Transfer to clean tea towel; rub briskly to remove as much of the skins as possible. Coarsely chop nuts; set aside.

In heatproof bowl over saucepan of simmering water, whisk together eggs, sugar and liqueur, whisking constantly until thick enough to coat back of spoon and instant-read thermometer reads 140°F (60°C), about 7 minutes. Whisk in white chocolate until melted and smooth. Remove bowl from heat; let cool.

Whip cream; fold one-third into white chocolate mixture. Fold in remaining whipped cream. Fold in all but 2 tbsp of the hazelnuts; spoon into prepared crust. Sprinkle with remaining hazelnuts. Freeze until firm, about 4 hours. *(Make-ahead: Cover with plastic wrap and overwrap with heavy-duty foil; freeze for up to 1 month. Thaw in refrigerator for 30 minutes before serving.)*

NUTRITIONAL INFORMATION, PER SERVING: about 577 cal, 8 g pro, 39 g total fat (19 g sat. fat), 49 g carb, 2 g fibre, 126 mg chol, 204 mg sodium. % RDI: 10% calcium, 13% iron, 24% vit A, 2% vit C, 20% folate.

Chocolate Walnut Tart

HANDS-ON TIME	TOTAL TIME	MAKES
30 MINUTES	3¼ HOURS	8 TO 12 SERVINGS

What you need

½ cup	packed brown sugar
½ cup	corn syrup
1 tbsp	butter
1 tsp	cornstarch
1	egg
1 tsp	vanilla
2 cups	walnut halves
⅓ cup	chopped dried sour cherries or raisins
1	egg yolk

CHOCOLATE PASTRY:

¾ cup	butter, softened
½ cup	granulated sugar
1	egg
1 tsp	vanilla
1¾ cups	all-purpose flour
⅓ cup	cocoa powder
¼ tsp	baking powder
pinch	salt

How to make it

CHOCOLATE PASTRY: In large bowl, beat butter with sugar until fluffy; beat in egg and vanilla. Into separate bowl, sift together flour, cocoa powder, baking powder and salt; sift again. Stir into butter mixture in 2 additions to make soft dough. Working with small handfuls, press about two-thirds onto bottom and up side of 9-inch (23 cm) fluted tart pan with removable bottom.

Form remaining pastry into disc; between waxed paper, roll out to 9-inch (23 cm) circle. Using fluted pastry wheel or sharp knife, cut into 1-inch (2.5 cm) wide strips. Refrigerate strips and shell until firm, about 2 hours. *(Make-ahead: Cover and refrigerate for up to 24 hours.)*

In bowl, beat together brown sugar, corn syrup, butter and cornstarch until combined; beat in egg and vanilla. Stir in walnuts and cherries. Scrape into pastry shell.

Whisk egg yolk with 1 tbsp water; brush over pastry rim. Arrange pastry strips over filling, leaving ¼-inch (5 mm) space between each. Trim ends of strips even with rim of pan; press to adhere to rim. Brush strips with egg mixture. Bake on bottom rack in 375°F (190°C) oven until pastry is firm and edges are darkened, about 40 minutes.

Let cool in pan on rack. *(Make-ahead: Cover and store for up to 24 hours.)*

Cut into wedges.

NUTRITIONAL INFORMATION, PER EACH OF 12 SERVINGS:
about 438 cal, 7 g pro, 26 g total fat (9 g sat. fat), 49 g carb, 3 g fibre, 87 mg chol, 166 mg sodium. % RDI: 5% calcium, 15% iron, 15% vit A, 22% folate.

Chocolate Walnut Fudge Scones

HANDS-ON TIME
30 MINUTES

TOTAL TIME
2¼ HOURS

MAKES
12 SCONES

What you need

2 cups	all-purpose flour
½ cup	cocoa powder
¼ cup	packed brown sugar
2½ tsp	baking powder
½ tsp	each baking soda and salt
½ cup	cold butter, cubed
1 cup	buttermilk
1	egg
1 tsp	vanilla
¾ cup	chopped toasted walnuts

FUDGE ICING:

1 cup	icing sugar
2 tbsp	cocoa powder
2 tbsp	milk (approx)
1 tsp	vanilla

How to make it

In large bowl, whisk together flour, cocoa powder, brown sugar, baking powder, baking soda and salt. Using pastry blender or 2 knives, cut in butter until in coarse crumbs. Whisk together buttermilk, egg and vanilla; add to flour mixture. Sprinkle with walnuts; stir with fork to make soft dough.

With floured hands, press dough into ball. On floured surface, knead gently 10 times. Pat into 10- x 7-inch (25 x 18 cm) rectangle; trim edges to straighten. Cut into 6 squares; cut each diagonally in half. Place on parchment paper–lined large rimless baking sheet. Bake in 400°F (200°C) oven until tops are firm to the touch, 18 to 20 minutes. Transfer to rack; let cool.

FUDGE ICING: In bowl, whisk icing sugar with cocoa powder. Add milk and vanilla; whisk until smooth, adding up to 1 tsp more milk if necessary to make spreadable. Spread over scones; let stand until set, about 1 hour. *(Make-ahead: Store in airtight container for up to 24 hours or wrap individually in plastic wrap and freeze in airtight container for up to 2 weeks.)*

NUTRITIONAL INFORMATION, PER SCONE: about 270 cal, 5 g pro, 14 g total fat (6 g sat. fat), 34 g carb, 2 g fibre, 41 mg chol, 307 mg sodium. % RDI: 7% calcium, 15% iron, 8% vit A, 17% folate.

Dark Chocolate and Dried Cherry Scones

HANDS-ON TIME	TOTAL TIME	MAKES
15 MINUTES	20 MINUTES	10 SCONES

What you need

¾ cup	whipping cream (35%)
2	eggs
1 tbsp	granulated sugar
2½ cups	all-purpose flour
4 tsp	baking powder
¼ tsp	salt
⅓ cup	cold butter, cubed
½ cup	dried sour cherries
½ cup	dark chocolate chips

TOPPING:

1 tbsp	whipping cream (35%)
1 tbsp	granulated sugar

How to make it

Whisk together cream, eggs and sugar. Set aside. In large bowl, whisk together flour, baking powder and salt. Using pastry blender or 2 knives, cut in butter until in coarse crumbs with a few larger pieces. Stir in cherries and chocolate chips. Using fork, stir in cream mixture to form soft dough.

Turn out onto lightly floured surface; knead gently once or twice until dough comes together. Pat out to scant ¾-inch (2 cm) thickness. Using floured 3-inch (8 cm) round cutter, cut out rounds, rerolling and cutting scraps once. Place, 1 inch (2.5 cm) apart, on parchment paper–lined rimless baking sheet.

TOPPING: Brush scones with cream; sprinkle with sugar. Bake in 450°F (230°C) oven until tops are light golden, about 12 minutes. Serve warm.

TIP FROM THE TEST KITCHEN

To ensure flaky results in pastries, it's vital that the fat stay cold and unmelted as it's cut into the flour mixture. The crumbs of flour-coated butter or lard melt in the oven, producing steam and lifting the layers apart. Handle the fat as little as possible when you're cubing it—the heat from your hands can melt it, so use a spoon or knife to scrape the cubes into the flour mixture.

NUTRITIONAL INFORMATION, PER SCONE: about 324 cal, 6 g pro, 17 g total fat (10 g sat. fat), 37 g carb, 2 g fibre, 77 mg chol, 201 mg sodium, 136 mg potassium. % RDI: 9% calcium, 16% iron, 14% vit A, 31% folate.

Spicy Chocolate Cinnamon Shortbread

HANDS-ON TIME	TOTAL TIME	MAKES
35 MINUTES	2½ HOURS	ABOUT 70 COOKIES

What you need

85 g	bittersweet chocolate, chopped
1 cup	unsalted butter, softened
⅓ cup	granulated sugar
½ tsp	vanilla
2¼ cups	all-purpose flour
¼ cup	cocoa powder
2 tbsp	cornstarch
1 tsp	cinnamon
¼ tsp	each nutmeg, salt and pepper
⅛ tsp	cayenne pepper

TOPPING:

140 g	bittersweet chocolate, chopped

How to make it

In heatproof bowl over saucepan of hot (not boiling) water, melt chocolate, stirring occasionally until smooth. Remove from heat; let cool.

In bowl, beat butter with sugar until fluffy; beat in melted chocolate and vanilla until smooth. Sift flour, cocoa powder, cornstarch, cinnamon, nutmeg, salt, pepper and cayenne pepper over butter mixture; stir to make smooth dough.

Between lightly floured waxed paper, roll out dough to ¼-inch (5 mm) thickness. With 2-inch (5 cm) teardrop-shaped cutter, cut out shapes, rerolling and cutting scraps. Place, about 1 inch (2.5 cm) apart, on parchment paper–lined rimless baking sheets. Refrigerate until firm, about 20 minutes.

Bake in 325°F (160°C) oven until firm, about 20 minutes. Let cool on pans on racks for 5 minutes. Transfer cookies to racks; let cool completely.

TOPPING: In heatproof bowl over saucepan of hot (not boiling) water, melt chocolate, stirring until smooth. Dip half of each cookie into chocolate on diagonal, shaking off excess. Place on waxed paper–lined baking sheets. Refrigerate until set, about 30 minutes.

TIP FROM THE TEST KITCHEN

The Canadian Living Test Kitchen uses salted butter in many baking recipes. If the ingredient list says simply "butter," we mean salted. However, this shortbread calls for unsalted butter which lends to the delicate, sweet flavour of the cookies.

NUTRITIONAL INFORMATION, PER COOKIE: about 62 cal, 1 g pro, 4 g total fat (2 g sat. fat), 6 g carb, 1 g fibre, 7 mg chol, 9 mg sodium, 13 mg potassium. % RDI: 3% iron, 2% vit A, 4% folate.

Chocolate and
Salted Caramel Swirl Ice Cream

HANDS-ON TIME	TOTAL TIME	MAKES
45 MINUTES	8 HOURS	ABOUT 4 CUPS

What you need

2 cups	milk
4 tsp	cornstarch
1½ cups	whipping cream (35%)
55 g	70% dark chocolate, chopped
¾ cup	granulated sugar
½ cup	cocoa powder
1 tsp	vanilla

SALTED CARAMEL SAUCE:

½ cup	granulated sugar
½ cup	whipping cream (35%)
½ tsp	salt

How to make it

Stir ¼ cup of the milk with cornstarch until dissolved; set aside.

In small saucepan, heat ½ cup of the cream with chocolate over low heat, stirring occasionally, just until melted and smooth, about 5 minutes. Remove from heat; set aside.

Meanwhile, in heavy-bottom saucepan, whisk together remaining milk and cream, sugar, cocoa powder and vanilla. Bring to boil over medium-high heat, stirring often; reduce heat to medium and cook, stirring, for 4 minutes. Stir in cornstarch mixture; cook, stirring, until thickened, 2 to 3 minutes.

Stir in chocolate mixture until smooth. Pour into 9-inch (2.5 L) square cake pan; place plastic wrap directly on surface. Refrigerate until chilled, about 1½ hours. *(Make-ahead: Transfer to airtight container; place plastic wrap directly on surface and refrigerate for up to 24 hours.)*

Transfer to freezer container and freeze until firm but not solid, 2 to 3 hours.

SALTED CARAMEL SAUCE: Meanwhile, in small deep saucepan over medium-high heat, stir sugar with ¼ cup water until dissolved, brushing down side of pan with pastry brush dipped in cold water. Bring to boil; boil vigorously, without stirring but brushing down side of pan often, until dark amber, about 6 minutes.

Standing back and averting face, add cream and salt; cook, stirring, until smooth and slightly thickened, about 2 minutes. Transfer to heatproof bowl; let stand until room temperature, about 1½ hours.

Scrape ice cream into food processor; purée until smooth. Spoon alternating layers of puréed ice cream and caramel sauce into freezer container, swirling with tip of knife or skewer. Cover and freeze until firm, about 4 hours.

NUTRITIONAL INFORMATION, PER ½ CUP: about 406 cal, 5 g pro, 26 g total fat (16 g sat. fat), 43 g carb, 2 g fibre, 82 mg chol, 192 mg sodium, 327 mg potassium. % RDI: 11% calcium, 12% iron, 22% vit A, 2% folate.

Chilly

Chocolate Sorbet

HANDS-ON TIME	TOTAL TIME	MAKES
10 MINUTES	7¼ HOURS	3 CUPS

What you need

¾ cup	granulated sugar
¼ cup	cocoa powder
1	slice fresh ginger
210 g	dark chocolate, chopped
55 g	milk chocolate, chopped

How to make it

In saucepan, bring sugar, cocoa powder, ginger and 2 cups water to boil over medium-high heat; boil, uncovered, for 5 minutes. Remove from heat; discard ginger.

Add dark and milk chocolates; whisk until smooth. Strain into 9-inch (2.5 L) square cake pan. Cover and refrigerate until cold, about 1½ hours.

Freeze until almost solid, about 1½ hours. Break up and purée in food processor until smooth. Scrape into airtight container; freeze until firm, about 4 hours. Or freeze in ice-cream machine according to manufacturer's instructions. (Make-ahead: Freeze for up to 1 week.)

NUTRITIONAL INFORMATION, PER ½ CUP: about 325 cal, 5 g pro, 22 g total fat (13 g sat. fat), 42 g carb, 6 g fibre, 2 mg chol, 16 mg sodium. % RDI: 4% calcium, 20% iron, 1% vit A, 2% folate.

Chocolate Chip Ice Cream Sandwiches

HANDS-ON TIME	TOTAL TIME	MAKES
20 MINUTES	4½ HOURS	8 SERVINGS

What you need

4 cups	chocolate ice cream, softened
1 cup	mini semisweet chocolate chips

CHOCOLATE CHIP COOKIES:

1 cup	butter, softened
1¼ cups	packed brown sugar
1	egg
1 tsp	vanilla
2 cups	all-purpose flour
1 tsp	baking soda
¼ tsp	salt
2 cups	semisweet chocolate chips
1 cup	chopped toasted pecans (optional)

How to make it

CHOCOLATE CHIP COOKIES: In bowl, beat butter with brown sugar until fluffy; beat in egg and vanilla. Whisk together flour, baking soda and salt. Stir into butter mixture. Stir in chocolate chips, and pecans (if using).

Drop by ¼ cup, about 2 inches (5 cm) apart, onto 2 parchment paper–lined or greased rimless baking sheets to make 16 cookies. Bake on top and bottom racks in 350°F (180°C) oven, rotating and switching pans halfway through, until bottoms are golden, about 15 minutes.

Let cool on pans on racks for 3 minutes. Transfer to racks; let cool completely. (*Make-ahead: Layer between waxed paper in airtight container and store for up to 5 days or freeze for up to 2 weeks.*)

Spread ½ cup ice cream on bottom of each of half of the cookies. Top with remaining cookies, pressing gently to spread ice cream to edge.

Roll edge of each sandwich in chocolate chips. Wrap individually in plastic wrap and freeze in airtight container until firm, about 4 hours. (*Make-ahead: Freeze for up to 5 days.*)

VARIATION
Vanilla Candy Ice Cream Sandwiches
Replace chocolate ice cream with vanilla ice cream; replace mini chocolate chips with mini coloured chocolate chips.

NUTRITIONAL INFORMATION, PER SERVING: about 928 cal, 10 g pro, 48 g total fat (29 g sat. fat), 118 g carb, 6 g fibre, 118 mg chol, 526 mg sodium. % RDI: 12% calcium, 34% iron, 31% vit A, 32% folate.

Sublime Brownies and Bourbon Sauce Sundaes

HANDS-ON TIME	TOTAL TIME	MAKES
35 MINUTES	1 HOUR	8 SERVINGS

What you need

85 g	bittersweet chocolate, chopped
55 g	unsweetened chocolate, chopped
⅓ cup	butter
¾ cup	granulated sugar
2	eggs
2 tsp	vanilla
½ cup	all-purpose flour
pinch	salt
3 cups	butter pecan ice cream

BOURBON SAUCE:

1½ cups	granulated sugar
⅔ cup	whipping cream (35%)
¼ cup	bourbon
1 tsp	lemon juice

How to make it

BOURBON SAUCE: In heavy saucepan over medium heat, stir sugar with ⅓ cup water until dissolved, brushing down side of pan with pastry brush dipped in cold water. Bring to boil; boil vigorously, without stirring but brushing down side of pan often, until dark amber, about 6 minutes. Standing back and averting face, add cream; whisk until smooth. Whisk in bourbon and lemon juice. Return pan to heat; simmer for 4 minutes. (*Make-ahead: Let cool; refrigerate in airtight container for up to 1 week. Gently rewarm to liquefy.*)

In heavy saucepan, melt together bittersweet chocolate, unsweetened chocolate and butter, stirring until smooth. Scrape into large bowl; let cool slightly.

Whisk in sugar; whisk in eggs, 1 at a time. Whisk in vanilla. Using wooden spoon, stir in flour and salt. Divide among 8 greased or paper-lined muffin cups, smoothing tops.

Bake in 350°F (180°C) oven just until cake tester inserted in centre of several comes out with a few moist crumbs clinging, about 25 minutes.

Let cool in pan on rack for 2 minutes. Transfer to rack; let cool slightly. (*Make-ahead: Let cool completely. Store in airtight container for up to 24 hours. To serve, place brownies on plate; cover and microwave on medium until softened and warm, about 1 minute.*)

Divide ¾ cup bourbon sauce among dessert plates (save remaining bourbon sauce for another use). Arrange brownie on each plate over sauce; top with ice cream.

NUTRITIONAL INFORMATION, PER SERVING: about 540 cal, 6 g pro, 30 g total fat (16 g sat. fat), 66 g carb, 2 g fibre, 105 mg chol, 182 mg sodium. % RDI: 10% calcium, 10% iron, 16% vit A, 8% folate.

Three–Ice Cream Terrine

HANDS-ON TIME	TOTAL TIME	MAKES
20 MINUTES	7½ HOURS	12 SERVINGS

What you need

2 cups	cubed (½ inch/1 cm) brownies
2 cups	chocolate ice cream, softened
2 cups	coffee ice cream, softened
2 cups	vanilla ice cream, softened

MOCHA SAUCE:

1 tbsp	instant coffee granules
⅓ cup	granulated sugar
⅓ cup	corn syrup
½ cup	whipping cream (35%)
170 g	bittersweet chocolate, chopped

How to make it

Line 8- x 4-inch (1.5 L) loaf pan with plastic wrap, leaving 3-inch (8 cm) overhang. Sprinkle half of the brownies evenly in pan; press gently to pack. Spread chocolate ice cream over brownies in pan, smoothing top; freeze until firm, about 2 hours.

Spread coffee ice cream over chocolate ice cream, smoothing top; freeze until firm, about 2 hours.

Spread vanilla ice cream over coffee ice cream, smoothing top. Sprinkle with remaining brownies; press gently. Fold plastic overhang over top; freeze until firm, about 2 hours. *(Make-ahead: Overwrap with heavy-duty foil and freeze for up to 1 week.)*

MOCHA SAUCE: In small saucepan, dissolve coffee granules in ⅓ cup water; stir in sugar and corn syrup. Bring to boil; cook, stirring, for 1 minute. Add cream and chocolate; cook, stirring, over medium heat until melted and smooth, about 2 minutes. Let cool. *(Make-ahead: Refrigerate in airtight container for up to 1 week. To reheat, microwave on medium-high for 1 minute.)*

Turn terrine out onto chilled serving plate; peel off plastic wrap. Let stand in refrigerator until soft enough to slice, about 15 minutes. Serve slices with mocha sauce.

VARIATION

Chocolate Fudge Sauce

Omit instant coffee granules from mocha fudge sauce.

NUTRITIONAL INFORMATION, PER SERVING: about 297 cal, 4 g pro, 19 g total fat (11 g sat. fat), 35 g carb, 3 g fibre, 37 mg chol, 76 mg sodium. % RDI: 9% calcium, 10% iron, 14% vit A, 5% vit C, 6% folate.

Mint Chocolate Chip Ice Cream Pie

HANDS-ON TIME	TOTAL TIME	MAKES
20 MINUTES	2½ HOURS	12 SERVINGS

What you need

2 cups	chocolate wafer crumbs
⅓ cup	butter, melted
⅓ cup	chocolate sauce
4 cups	mint chocolate chip ice cream, softened
¾ cup	whipping cream (35%)
1 tbsp	granulated sugar
2 tsp	chocolate shot (see tip, page 87)

How to make it

Stir chocolate wafer crumbs with butter until moistened; press over bottom and up side of 9-inch (23 cm) pie plate. Bake in 325°F (160°C) oven until firm, about 12 minutes. Let cool.

Spread chocolate sauce over crust. Using wooden spoon, beat ice cream until smooth; spread over chocolate sauce. Cover with plastic wrap; freeze until firm, about 1 hour.

Whip cream with sugar; spread over ice cream. Freeze until set, about 1 hour.

Garnish with chocolate shot. *(Make-ahead: Cover with plastic wrap and overwrap with heavy-duty foil; freeze for up to 1 day.)*

TIP FROM THE TEST KITCHEN

Chocolate wafer crumbs are easy to find in the baking aisle of the grocery store, but it's not hard to make them at home: Choose thin chocolate wafer cookies without any cream filling, break them up and pulse them in the food processor until fine but not powdery.

NUTRITIONAL INFORMATION, PER SERVING: about 302 cal, 4 g pro, 19 g total fat (11 g sat. fat), 32 g carb, 1 g fibre, 50 mg chol, 213 mg sodium. % RDI: 7% calcium, 8% iron, 15% vit A, 7% folate.

Mini Baked Alaskas

HANDS-ON TIME	**TOTAL TIME**	**MAKES**
20 MINUTES	5¼ HOURS	6 SERVINGS

What you need

6	round (about 2 inch/5 cm) chocolate wafer cookies
6	scoops (each ⅓ cup) premium-quality chocolate ice cream
3	egg whites
½ cup	granulated sugar

How to make it

On parchment paper–lined rimmed baking sheet, top each cookie with 1 scoop of the ice cream. Freeze for 1 hour.

In bowl, beat egg whites until soft peaks form. Beat in sugar, 1 tbsp at a time, until stiff peaks form.

Using piping bag fitted with star tip, pipe meringue over ice cream to cover completely, ensuring that meringue seals to cookie. Freeze until firm, about 4 hours.

Bake in 500°F (260°C) oven until browned, about 2 minutes. Serve immediately.

TIP FROM THE TEST KITCHEN

Beating air into egg whites gives them height and structure. The secret to success is to start with a perfectly clean metal or glass bowl and use a big wire whisk. (A stand mixer with a whisk attachment makes this process faster.) Beat just until you see the results you want, then stop. For "soft peaks," you're looking for peaks that droop when you lift out the whisk. "Stiff peaks" are glossy and stand tall when you lift out the whisk. If you're incorporating sugar into the egg whites to achieve firm peaks, add it 1 to 2 tbsp at a time, beating the mixture continuously.

NUTRITIONAL INFORMATION, PER SERVING: about 298 cal, 5 g pro, 14 g total fat (8 g sat. fat), 38 g carb, 2 g fibre, 70 mg chol, 97 mg sodium. % RDI: 6% calcium, 9% iron, 10% vit A, 1% folate.

Neapolitan Pistachio Frozen Bombe

HANDS-ON TIME	TOTAL TIME	MAKES
1 HOUR	5¼ HOURS	8 TO 12 SERVINGS

What you need

3 cups	chocolate ice cream
2 cups	strawberry ice cream
170 g	semisweet chocolate, chopped
¾ cup	whipping cream (35%)
½ cup	chopped pistachios

CAKE:

1	egg
1	egg yolk
¼ cup	granulated sugar
1 tsp	vanilla
¼ cup	all-purpose flour
¼ tsp	baking powder
pinch	salt
1 tbsp	butter, melted
2 tbsp	finely chopped pistachios

How to make it

CAKE: In bowl, beat egg with egg yolk until foamy. Beat in sugar, 2 tbsp at a time, until batter falls in ribbons when beaters are lifted, about 3 minutes. Beat in vanilla. Whisk together flour, baking powder and salt; sift half over egg mixture and fold in. Repeat with remaining flour mixture.

Transfer one-quarter of the batter to small bowl; fold in butter. Pour back over batter; sprinkle with pistachios and fold in. Scrape into greased 8-inch (2 L) springform pan.

Bake in 325°F (160°C) oven until cake springs back when lightly touched, about 30 minutes. Let cool in pan on rack for 10 minutes. Turn cake out onto rack; let cool completely.

Let chocolate and strawberry ice creams stand at room temperature until soft enough to scoop, 20 minutes.

Dampen 7½-inch (1.5 L) bowl; line with plastic wrap, leaving 3-inch (8 cm) overhang. Line bowl with strawberry ice cream, spreading in even layer. Fill with chocolate ice cream, smoothing top. Trim cake to fit bowl; place over ice cream, pressing gently. Cover with plastic wrap; freeze until firm, about 3 hours. (*Make-ahead: Freeze for up to 24 hours.*)

Place chocolate in heatproof bowl. In small saucepan, bring cream just to boil; pour over chocolate, whisking until smooth. Let cool for 10 minutes.

Remove plastic wrap from top of bombe. Invert bowl onto rack over rimmed baking sheet; remove bowl and peel off plastic wrap. Starting at top of dome, pour chocolate mixture over cake in spiral motion, spreading with palette knife to cover completely and letting excess drip off. Sprinkle bottom edge with pistachios. Freeze until set, about 15 minutes. (*Make-ahead: Wrap in plastic wrap and overwrap with heavy-duty foil; freeze for up to 2 weeks.*)

Transfer bombe to chilled flat serving plate. Let stand in refrigerator for 10 minutes before cutting into wedges.

NUTRITIONAL INFORMATION, PER EACH OF 12 SERVINGS: about 316 cal, 5 g pro, 21 g total fat (11 g sat. fat), 32 g carb, 2 g fibre, 79 mg chol, 71 mg sodium. % RDI: 9% calcium, 10% iron, 14% vit A, 2% vit C, 8% folate.

Frozen Banana Bites

HANDS-ON TIME
20 MINUTES

TOTAL TIME
1¼ HOURS

MAKES
ABOUT 16 PIECES

What you need

¾ cup	semisweet chocolate chips
2 tsp	vegetable oil
¼ cup	sweetened flaked coconut, toasted
¼ cup	salted roasted peanuts
2	large bananas, cut in ½-inch (1 cm) thick slices

How to make it

In heatproof bowl over saucepan of hot (not boiling) water, melt chocolate chips, stirring until smooth. Stir in oil.

Place coconut and peanuts in separate shallow bowls.

Using fork, dip banana slices into chocolate, turning to coat and letting excess drip back into bowl.

Using clean fork, roll banana slices in coconut and/or peanuts; place on parchment paper–lined baking sheet. Spear each banana slice with toothpick.

Freeze until chocolate is set and banana is frozen, about 1 hour. *(Make-ahead: Cover and freeze for up to 3 days.)*

TIP FROM THE TEST KITCHEN
This recipe requires bananas that are ripe but firm so that the frozen slices stand up to dipping and handling. Look for peels that are yellow but not yet speckled with brown.

NUTRITIONAL INFORMATION, PER PIECE: about 81 cal, 1 g pro, 5 g total fat (2 g sat. fat), 10 g carb, 1 g fibre, 0 mg chol, 16 mg sodium, 111 mg potassium. % RDI: 1% calcium, 3% iron, 2% vit C, 3% folate.

Neapolitan Milkshake

HANDS-ON TIME	TOTAL TIME	MAKES
5 MINUTES	45 MINUTES	1 SERVING

What you need

½ cup	vanilla ice cream
⅓ cup	2% milk
½ cup	chocolate ice cream
3 tbsp	1% chocolate milk
½ cup	strawberry ice cream

How to make it

In blender, purée vanilla ice cream with half of the 2% milk until smooth. Pour into tall glass; freeze until almost firm, about 20 minutes.

In blender, purée chocolate ice cream with chocolate milk until smooth. Spoon over vanilla layer; freeze until almost firm, about 20 minutes.

In blender, purée strawberry ice cream with remaining 2% milk until smooth. Spoon over chocolate layer. Serve immediately.

NUTRITIONAL INFORMATION, PER SERVING: about 652 cal, 14 g pro, 38 g total fat (23 g sat. fat), 66 g carb, 1 g fibre, 170 mg chol, 214 mg sodium, 661 mg potassium. % RDI: 42% calcium, 10% iron, 48% vit A, 10% vit C, 12% folate.

Moustache Straw Cookies

HANDS-ON TIME	TOTAL TIME	MAKES
45 MINUTES	3 HOURS	ABOUT 40 COOKIES

What you need

¾ cup	butter, softened
1 cup	granulated sugar
1	egg
1 tsp	vanilla
2½ cups	all-purpose flour
½ tsp	baking powder
pinch	salt
⅓ cup	pasteurized egg whites
3½ cups	icing sugar
	brown paste food colouring

How to make it

In bowl, beat butter with sugar until fluffy; beat in egg and vanilla. Whisk flour, baking powder and salt; stir into butter mixture in 3 additions. Divide in half and shape into discs; wrap and refrigerate for 1 hour.

Let dough stand at room temperature for 15 minutes. Between parchment paper, roll out, 1 disc at a time, to ¼-inch (5 mm) thickness. Using floured cookie cutter, cut out shapes. Arrange, 1 inch (2.5 cm) apart, on parchment paper–lined rimless baking sheet. Using straw, cut hole in centre of each. Bake in 375°F (190°C) oven until light golden, 10 minutes. Recut holes; let cool on pan on rack for 1 minute. Transfer to rack; let cool completely.

In bowl, beat egg whites until foamy, 30 to 60 seconds. Beat in icing sugar, 1 cup at a time, until thick and glossy, 6 to 8 minutes. Tint with food colouring; pipe onto cookies.

NUTRITIONAL INFORMATION, PER COOKIE: about 161 cal, 2 g pro, 4 g total fat (2 g sat. fat), 31 g carb, trace fibre, 14 mg chol, 37 mg sodium, 16 mg potassium. % RDI: 3% iron, 3% vit A, 5% folate.

Chocolate Brownie Martini

HANDS-ON TIME	TOTAL TIME	MAKES
5 MINUTES	5 MINUTES	1 SERVING

What you need

	ice cubes
2 tbsp	vanilla vodka or vodka
2 tbsp	brown crème de cacao
1 tbsp	Frangelico
1 tbsp	whipping cream (35%)
	shaved dark chocolate

How to make it

Fill cocktail shaker with ice. Add vodka, crème de cacao, Frangelico and cream; shake vigorously to blend and chill.

Strain mixture into martini glass; garnish with shaved chocolate.

NUTRITIONAL INFORMATION, PER SERVING: about 279 cal, trace pro, 5 g total fat (3 g sat. fat), 24 g carb, 0 g fibre, 19 mg chol, 10 mg sodium, 25 mg potassium. % RDI: 1% calcium, 6% vit A.

Chocolate Mint Martini

HANDS-ON TIME	TOTAL TIME	MAKES
5 MINUTES	5 MINUTES	1 SERVING

What you need

	ice cubes
2 tbsp	vodka
2 tbsp	white crème de cacao
1 tbsp	white crème de menthe

GARNISH:

	white crème de menthe
	crushed candy canes or coarse red sugar

How to make it

GARNISH: Moisten rim of martini glass with crème de menthe; coat with candy cane.

Fill cocktail shaker with ice. Add vodka, crème de cacao and crème de menthe; shake vigorously to blend and chill.

Strain mixture into prepared martini glass.

NUTRITIONAL INFORMATION, PER SERVING: about 234 cal, trace pro, trace total fat (trace sat. fat), 22 g carb, 0 g fibre, 0 mg chol, 4 mg sodium, 10 mg potassium.

Double-Chocolate Semifreddo

HANDS-ON TIME	TOTAL TIME	MAKES
40 MINUTES	7½ HOURS	8 SERVINGS

What you need

170 g	white chocolate, chopped
170 g	milk chocolate, chopped
4	eggs
¼ cup	granulated sugar
1¾ cups	whipping cream (35%)

How to make it

Line 8- x 4-inch (1.5 L) loaf pan with plastic wrap, smoothing out any wrinkles. Set aside.

In separate heatproof bowls set over saucepan of hot (not boiling) water, melt white chocolate and milk chocolate, stirring until smooth. Let cool to room temperature.

In large heatproof bowl over saucepan of simmering water, beat eggs with sugar until consistency of softly whipped cream, about 5 minutes. Divide between 2 large bowls. Whisk white chocolate into 1 bowl; whisk milk chocolate into second bowl. Refrigerate until cold.

Whip cream. Divide half between white and milk chocolate mixtures; fold in. Fold one-third of the remaining whipped cream into milk chocolate mixture. Fold remaining whipped cream into white chocolate mixture.

Drop alternating spoonfuls of milk chocolate and white chocolate mixtures into prepared pan. Using knife, gently swirl. Place plastic wrap directly on surface; freeze until firm, about 6 hours. (*Make-ahead: Overwrap with heavy-duty foil and freeze for up to 1 week.*)

To serve, let soften in refrigerator for 30 minutes. Unwrap and invert onto serving platter. Peel off plastic wrap; slice.

TIP FROM THE TEST KITCHEN

When you beat the eggs with the sugar for this semifreddo, you want them to become fairly thick from the heat and the air that's being incorporated. The mixture should look like softly whipped cream; it should stand up slightly but any peaks should droop quickly.

NUTRITIONAL INFORMATION, PER SERVING: about 455 cal, 7 g pro, 34 g total fat (20 g sat. fat), 33 g carb, 1 g fibre, 169 mg chol, 86 mg sodium. % RDI: 12% calcium, 4% iron, 25% vit A, 9% folate.

Cakey

Chocolate Cherry Pancakes
With Cherry Syrup

HANDS-ON TIME	TOTAL TIME	MAKES
30 MINUTES	30 MINUTES	6 SERVINGS

What you need

1½ cups	all-purpose flour
3 tbsp	granulated sugar
1 tsp	each baking powder and baking soda
¼ tsp	salt
1¾ cups	buttermilk
1	egg
2 tbsp	butter, melted
2 tsp	vanilla
¾ cup	sweet cherries, pitted and halved
⅓ cup	dark chocolate chunks
1 tbsp	canola oil
½ cup	mascarpone cheese
2 tbsp	maple syrup

CHERRY SYRUP:

2 cups	sweet cherries, pitted and halved
½ cup	maple syrup
1 tsp	lemon juice

How to make it

CHERRY SYRUP: In saucepan, bring cherries and maple syrup to boil over medium-high heat; reduce heat and simmer, stirring often, until thickened, about 15 minutes. Stir in lemon juice. Set aside.

In large bowl, whisk together flour, sugar, baking powder, baking soda and salt. Whisk together buttermilk, egg, butter and 1 tsp of the vanilla; pour over dry ingredients and whisk until combined but still slightly lumpy. Fold in cherries and chocolate.

Lightly brush large nonstick skillet or griddle with some of the oil; heat over medium heat. Using scant ⅓ cup per pancake, pour in batter; spread slightly to form circles. Cook until bubbles appear on top, about 4 minutes. Flip and cook until bottoms are golden, about 1 minute. Transfer to baking sheet; cover and keep warm in 250°F (120°C) oven.

In bowl, stir together mascarpone cheese, maple syrup and remaining vanilla. Serve with pancakes and cherry syrup.

TIP FROM THE TEST KITCHEN

No buttermilk? For each 1 cup you need, pour 1 tbsp vinegar or lemon juice into a glass measuring cup and pour in enough milk to make 1 cup. Let the mixture stand for 5 minutes to thicken.

NUTRITIONAL INFORMATION, PER SERVING: about 244 cal, 5 g pro, 10 g total fat (5 g sat. fat), 34 g carb, 1 g fibre, 31 mg chol, 228 mg sodium, 199 mg potassium. % RDI: 8% calcium, 12% iron, 5% vit A, 3% vit C, 12% folate.

Mocha Snacking Cake

HANDS-ON TIME	TOTAL TIME	MAKES
10 MINUTES	1 HOUR	12 SERVINGS

What you need

⅔ cup	butter, softened
1½ cups	granulated sugar
2	eggs
1 tsp	vanilla
1⅔ cups	all-purpose flour
¾ cup	cocoa powder
1 tsp	baking soda
1 tsp	baking powder
¼ tsp	salt
1⅓ cups	strong brewed coffee, cooled

How to make it

Grease 8-inch (2 L) square cake pan; line bottom with parchment paper or waxed paper. Set aside.

In large bowl, beat butter with sugar until fluffy; beat in eggs, 1 at a time, just until incorporated. Stir in vanilla. Sift together flour, cocoa powder, baking soda, baking powder and salt; beat into butter mixture alternately with coffee, making 2 additions of flour mixture and 1 of coffee, until almost smooth. Pour into prepared pan; spread evenly and smooth top.

Bake in 350°F (180°C) oven until cake tester inserted in centre comes out clean, 45 to 50 minutes.

Let cool in pan on rack. (*Make-ahead: Wrap in plastic wrap and store for up to 3 days. Or overwrap with heavy-duty foil and freeze for up to 2 weeks.*)

TIP FROM THE TEST KITCHEN
If you don't have strong brewed coffee, mix 1⅓ cups boiling water with 2 tbsp instant coffee granules.

NUTRITIONAL INFORMATION, PER SERVING: about 275 cal, 4 g pro, 12 g total fat (7 g sat. fat), 41 g carb, 2 g fibre, 63 mg chol, 283 mg sodium. % RDI: 2% calcium, 13% iron, 11% vit A, 19% folate.

Sour Cream Chocolate Crumb Cake

HANDS-ON TIME		TOTAL TIME		MAKES
15 MINUTES		55 MINUTES		12 SERVINGS

What you need

½ cup	unsalted butter, softened
½ cup	granulated sugar
1	egg
1	egg yolk
1⅓ cups	all-purpose flour
½ tsp	baking soda
¼ tsp	salt
½ cup	sour cream
85 g	bittersweet chocolate, melted

TOPPING:

½ cup	packed brown sugar
¼ cup	granulated sugar
¼ tsp	cinnamon
pinch	salt
½ cup	unsalted butter, melted and warm
1⅓ cups	all-purpose flour
⅓ cup	ground almonds

How to make it

TOPPING: In bowl, stir together brown sugar, granulated sugar, cinnamon and salt; stir in butter. Stir in flour and almonds; using hands, press mixture together. Let cool.

In large bowl, beat butter with sugar until combined. Beat in egg and egg yolk. Whisk together flour, baking soda and salt. Stir into butter mixture alternately with sour cream, making 3 additions of flour mixture and 2 of sour cream. Stir in chocolate.

Spread in parchment paper–lined 8-inch (2 L) square cake pan. Crumble topping evenly over batter.

Bake in 350°F (180°C) oven until cake tester inserted in centre comes out clean, 35 to 40 minutes. Let cool in pan on rack.

VARIATION

Sour Cream Chocolate Chunk Crumb Cake

Substitute ⅓ cup chopped bittersweet chocolate for the melted chocolate.

TIP FROM THE TEST KITCHEN

A cake tester is a simple metal wire with a handle. It's a handy tool designed for checking the doneness of cakes. If you don't have one, a skewer or toothpick works just as well.

NUTRITIONAL INFORMATION, PER SERVING: about 387 cal, 5 g pro, 21 g total fat (12 g sat. fat), 46 g carb, 2 g fibre, 77 mg chol, 116 mg sodium, 105 mg potassium. % RDI: 4% calcium, 14% iron, 16% vit A, 29% folate.

Cakey Chocolate Brownies

HANDS-ON TIME	•	TOTAL TIME	•	MAKES
10 MINUTES		30 MINUTES		20 SQUARES

What you need

⅓ cup	butter, softened
1 cup	granulated sugar
3	eggs
1 tsp	vanilla
55 g	unsweetened chocolate, melted and cooled
55 g	bittersweet chocolate, melted and cooled
1 cup	all-purpose flour
½ tsp	baking powder
¼ tsp	salt

How to make it

In large bowl, beat butter with sugar until combined; beat in eggs, 1 at a time. Beat in vanilla; beat in unsweetened and bittersweet chocolates. Stir in flour, baking powder and salt. Spread in parchment paper–lined 8-inch (2 L) square cake pan.

Bake in 350°F (180°C) oven until cake tester inserted in centre comes out with a few moist crumbs clinging, about 20 minutes. Let cool in pan on rack. *(Make-ahead: Wrap and store for up to 2 days.)*

Cut into squares.

VARIATIONS

Cakey Chocolate Brownies With Coconut Pecan Icing

Bake brownies as directed. While brownies are cooling, in small saucepan over low heat, stir together ⅓ cup granulated sugar, ⅓ cup evaporated milk, 1 egg yolk and 2 tbsp butter. Cook, stirring constantly and without boiling, until thickened, about 8 minutes. Remove from heat. Stir in ¾ cup sweetened flaked coconut, ⅓ cup chopped toasted pecans and ½ tsp vanilla. Let cool. Spread over cooled brownies; cut into squares.

Cakey Chocolate Brownies With Chocolate Icing

Bake brownies as directed. While brownies are cooling, in bowl, beat 1 cup icing sugar with ¼ cup butter. Beat in 30 g unsweetened chocolate, melted and cooled; 4 tsp hot water; and ½ tsp vanilla until fluffy. Spread over cooled brownies; cut into squares.

NUTRITIONAL INFORMATION, PER SQUARE: about 130 cal, 2 g pro, 6 g total fat (4 g sat. fat), 17 g carb, 1 g fibre, 36 mg chol, 67 mg sodium. % RDI: 1% calcium, 6% iron, 4% vit A, 7% folate.

Chocolate Chocolate Loaf

HANDS-ON TIME	TOTAL TIME	MAKES
10 MINUTES	1½ HOURS	1 LOAF, OR 12 SLICES

What you need

½ cup	butter, softened
1¼ cups	packed brown sugar
2	eggs
2 tsp	vanilla
1¾ cups	all-purpose flour
¾ cup	cocoa powder
1 tsp	baking powder
½ tsp	each baking soda and salt
1 cup	sour cream
¾ cup	semisweet chocolate chips
¼ cup	chopped pecan halves

How to make it

In large bowl, beat butter with brown sugar until fluffy. Beat in eggs, 1 at a time; beat in vanilla. Sift together flour, cocoa powder, baking powder, baking soda and salt until no streaks remain; stir into butter mixture alternately with sour cream, making 2 additions of flour mixture and 1 of sour cream. Fold in chocolate chips and pecans. Scrape into parchment paper–lined or greased 9- x 5-inch (2 L) loaf pan.

Bake in 350°F (180°C) oven until cake tester inserted in centre comes out clean, about 70 minutes.

Transfer to rack; let cool completely. (*Make-ahead: Wrap in plastic wrap and store in airtight container for up to 3 days or overwrap with foil and freeze for up to 1 month.*)

NUTRITIONAL INFORMATION, PER SLICE: about 345 cal, 5 g pro, 16 g total fat (9 g sat. fat), 47 g carb, 3 g fibre, 63 mg chol, 273 mg sodium. % RDI: 6% calcium, 19% iron, 11% vit A, 22% folate.

Chocolate Strawberry Shortcake

HANDS-ON TIME	TOTAL TIME	MAKES
30 MINUTES	1½ HOURS	8 SERVINGS

What you need

3 cups	sliced strawberries
3 tbsp	granulated sugar
4 cups	vanilla ice cream
½ cup	chocolate sauce (such as Rich Double-Chocolate Sauce, page 25)

CHOCOLATE BISCUITS:

2¼ cups	all-purpose flour
½ cup	cocoa powder
½ cup	granulated sugar
2½ tsp	baking powder
½ tsp	each baking soda and salt
½ cup	cold unsalted butter, cubed
1 cup	buttermilk
1	egg
1 tsp	vanilla

TOPPING:

1 tbsp	whipping cream (35%)
2 tsp	granulated sugar

How to make it

CHOCOLATE BISCUITS: In large bowl, whisk together flour, cocoa powder, sugar, baking powder, baking soda and salt. Using pastry blender or 2 knives, cut in butter until crumbly. Whisk together buttermilk, egg and vanilla; add to flour mixture, stirring with fork to form soft dough.

With lightly floured hands, press dough into ball. On lightly floured surface, knead gently 10 times. Pat into 1-inch (2.5 cm) thick round. Using 3-inch (8 cm) round cookie cutter, cut out rounds, patting out and cutting scraps. Place on parchment paper–lined rimless baking sheet.

TOPPING: Brush biscuits with cream; sprinkle with sugar. Bake in 400°F (200°C) oven until puffed and cake tester inserted into several comes out clean, 15 to 20 minutes. Let cool on pan on rack. (*Make-ahead: Set aside for up to 6 hours.*)

Meanwhile, mix strawberries with sugar; cover and let stand until juicy, about 20 minutes. (*Make-ahead: Let stand for up to 2 hours.*)

Split biscuits horizontally in half; place bottom halves on plates. Layer with strawberries, ice cream and biscuit tops; drizzle chocolate sauce over tops.

NUTRITIONAL INFORMATION, PER SERVING: about 566 cal, 10 g pro, 24 g total fat (14 g sat. fat), 83 g carb, 5 g fibre, 88 mg chol, 474 mg sodium. % RDI: 20% calcium, 23% iron, 20% vit A, 62% vit C, 44% folate.

Hot Fudge Banana Bundt Cake

HANDS-ON TIME
30 MINUTES

TOTAL TIME
2 HOURS

MAKES
12 SERVINGS

What you need

1 cup	unsalted butter, softened
1¾ cups	granulated sugar
6	eggs
3 cups	all-purpose flour
1½ tsp	baking powder
¾ tsp	baking soda
¾ tsp	salt
1½ cups	mashed bananas (about 5 small)
1½ tsp	vinegar

HOT FUDGE SAUCE:

1½ cups	whipping cream (35%)
1¼ cups	granulated sugar
115 g	unsweetened chocolate, coarsely chopped
55 g	bittersweet chocolate, coarsely chopped
2 tbsp	butter
2 tbsp	corn syrup
½ tsp	vanilla

How to make it

HOT FUDGE SAUCE: In heavy saucepan, combine cream, sugar, unsweetened chocolate, bittersweet chocolate, butter and corn syrup; heat over low heat, whisking constantly, until sugar is dissolved and chocolate is melted. Boil over medium-high heat, whisking constantly, until reduced to 2½ cups, about 8 minutes. Let cool until room temperature but still pourable. *(Make-ahead: Refrigerate in airtight container for up to 1 week; gently rewarm to liquefy.)* Stir in vanilla.

In bowl, beat butter with sugar until light and fluffy. Beat in eggs, 1 at a time, beating well after each. Whisk together flour, baking powder, baking soda and salt. Stir bananas with vinegar. Stir flour mixture into egg mixture alternately with banana mixture, making 3 additions of flour mixture and 2 of banana mixture.

Pour one-quarter of the batter into greased and floured 10-inch (3 L) Bundt pan; leaving ½-inch (1 cm) border around edge of pan, drizzle ¼ cup of the fudge sauce over batter. Repeat layers twice. Top with remaining batter. Run thin knife or skewer through batter to create swirls. Bake in 350°F (180°C) oven until cake tester inserted in centre comes out clean, about 1 hour.

Let cool in pan on rack for 30 minutes. Invert pan onto rack; remove pan. Let cool completely. *(Make-ahead: Wrap in plastic wrap and store for up to 2 days or overwrap in heavy-duty foil and freeze for up to 2 weeks.)*

Serve thick slices with remaining fudge sauce.

NUTRITIONAL INFORMATION, PER SERVING: about 704 cal, 9 g pro, 38 g total fat (23 g sat. fat), 88 g carb, 4 g fibre, 192 mg chol, 320 mg sodium. % RDI: 6% calcium, 19% iron, 31% vit A, 3% vit C, 21% folate.

Chocolate Chip Angel Food Cake

HANDS-ON TIME
40 MINUTES

TOTAL TIME
2 HOURS

MAKES
12 SERVINGS

What you need

1¼ cups	sifted cake-and-pastry flour
1½ cups	granulated sugar
1½ cups	egg whites (about 11)
1 tbsp	lemon juice
1 tsp	cream of tartar
½ tsp	salt
½ cup	mini semisweet chocolate chips or regular semisweet chocolate chips
2 tsp	vanilla

GLAZE:

55 g	bittersweet chocolate, coarsely chopped
⅓ cup	whipping cream (35%)
1 tsp	corn syrup

How to make it

Into bowl, sift flour with ¾ cup of the sugar; sift again into separate bowl. Set aside.

In large bowl, beat egg whites until foamy. Add lemon juice, cream of tartar and salt; beat until soft peaks form. Beat in remaining sugar, 2 tbsp at a time, until stiff glossy peaks form. Sift flour mixture over top, one-quarter at a time, gently folding in each addition until blended. Fold in chocolate chips and vanilla.

Pour into ungreased 10-inch (4 L) tube pan. Run spatula through batter to eliminate any large air bubbles; smooth top. Bake in 350°F (180°C) oven until cake springs back when lightly touched, 45 to 50 minutes.

Turn pan upside down and let hang on legs attached to pan or on bottle until cooled. Remove from pan; invert onto cake plate. *(Make-ahead: Wrap with plastic wrap and store in airtight container for up to 2 days or overwrap with foil and freeze for up to 1 month.)*

GLAZE: In heatproof bowl over saucepan of hot (not boiling) water, melt chocolate. Stir in cream and corn syrup until smooth. Spread over top of cake, letting drip down side. *(Make-ahead: Cover loosely in plastic wrap and store for up to 24 hours.)*

NUTRITIONAL INFORMATION, PER SERVING: about 239 cal, 5 g pro, 7 g total fat (4 g sat. fat), 41 g carb, 1 g fibre, 9 mg chol, 148 mg sodium. % RDI: 1% calcium, 10% iron, 2% vit A, 7% folate.

Dairy-Free Chocolate and Olive Oil Bundt Cake With Chocolate Sauce

HANDS-ON TIME	TOTAL TIME	MAKES
25 MINUTES	1½ HOURS	8 TO 10 SERVINGS

What you need

1¼ cups	all-purpose flour
¾ cup	cocoa powder, sifted
¼ cup	ground almonds
1½ tsp	baking powder
¾ tsp	baking soda
½ tsp	salt
1¼ cups	packed brown sugar
1 cup	olive oil
3	eggs
1 tbsp	lemon juice
½ cup	sliced almonds
2 tsp	icing sugar

CHOCOLATE SAUCE:

½ cup	soy milk
3 tbsp	corn syrup
140 g	70% dark chocolate, finely chopped
1 tbsp	dairy-free butter-flavoured spread (such as Earth Balance)
¼ tsp	vanilla

How to make it

In bowl, whisk together flour, cocoa powder, ground almonds, baking powder, baking soda and salt. Remove 2 tbsp and use to flour greased 10-cup (2.5 L) fancy Bundt pan.

In large bowl, beat together brown sugar, oil, eggs, ⅓ cup water and lemon juice; stir in remaining flour mixture until combined. Stir in sliced almonds. Scrape into prepared pan.

Bake in 325°F (160°C) oven until cake tester inserted in centre comes out clean, about 55 minutes. Invert onto rack; remove pan. Let cool completely. (*Make-ahead: Wrap in plastic wrap and store for up to 2 days or freeze in airtight container for up to 2 weeks.*) Dust with icing sugar.

CHOCOLATE SAUCE: In saucepan, bring soy milk and corn syrup to boil. Remove from heat; whisk in chocolate, butter-flavoured spread and vanilla until melted and smooth. Let cool slightly. Serve with cake.

TIP FROM THE TEST KITCHEN

Fancy Bundt pans come in all sorts of shapes, including stars, flowers and cathedral windows. But if you don't have one, a regular Bundt pan or any 10-cup (3 L) tube-shaped pan will work just fine for this cake.

NUTRITIONAL INFORMATION, PER EACH OF 10 SERVINGS: about 544 cal, 8 g pro, 35 g total fat (8 g sat. fat), 56 g carb, 5 g fibre, 55 mg chol, 313 mg sodium, 401 mg potassium. % RDI: 9% calcium, 31% iron, 5% vit A, 17% folate.

Glazed Double-Chocolate Marble Cake

HANDS-ON TIME	TOTAL TIME	MAKES
30 MINUTES	3¼ HOURS	16 SERVINGS

What you need

55 g	unsweetened chocolate, chopped
85 g	white chocolate, chopped
⅔ cup	butter, softened
1½ cups	granulated sugar
3	eggs
2 tsp	vanilla
2¼ cups	all-purpose flour
1 tsp	each baking powder and baking soda
½ tsp	salt
1 cup	buttermilk
	white chocolate shards (optional)

GANACHE:

55 g	bittersweet chocolate, chopped
¼ cup	whipping cream (35%)

How to make it

In separate bowls over saucepan of hot (not boiling) water, melt unsweetened chocolate and white chocolate, stirring occasionally until smooth; let cool to room temperature.

In large bowl, beat butter with sugar until fluffy. Beat in eggs, 1 at a time, beating well after each. Beat in vanilla.

Spoon half of the butter mixture into separate bowl; stir in unsweetened chocolate. Stir white chocolate into remaining butter mixture.

Whisk together flour, baking powder, baking soda and salt. Stir half into dark chocolate mixture alternately with half of the buttermilk, making 2 additions of flour mixture and 1 of buttermilk. Repeat with white chocolate mixture, remaining flour mixture and buttermilk.

Drop spoonfuls of dark and white batters into greased and floured 10-cup (2.5 L) fancy or classic Bundt or tube pan. With tip of knife, swirl batters to marble. Bake in 325°F (160°C) oven until cake tester inserted in centre comes out clean, about 55 minutes. Let cool in pan on rack for 10 minutes. Invert pan onto rack; remove pan. Let cool completely. *(Make-ahead: Wrap in plastic wrap and store for up to 1 day or overwrap with heavy-duty foil and freeze for up to 1 month.)*

GANACHE: Place bittersweet chocolate in heatproof bowl. In saucepan, bring cream just to boil; pour over chocolate, stirring until melted and smooth. Let stand for 10 minutes; brush over cake.

Sprinkle white chocolate shards (if using) over cake. Let stand until ganache is set, about 40 minutes. *(Make-ahead: Cover cake with bowl or place in airtight container and store for up to 1 day.)*

NUTRITIONAL INFORMATION, PER SERVING: about 304 cal, 5 g pro, 15 g total fat (9 g sat. fat), 39 g carb, 1 g fibre, 64 mg chol, 275 mg sodium. % RDI: 5% calcium, 9% iron, 10% vit A, 12% folate.

Chocolate Cupcakes With Double-Chocolate Icing

HANDS-ON TIME	•	TOTAL TIME	•	MAKES
30 MINUTES		1½ HOURS		12 CUPCAKES

What you need

55 g	bittersweet chocolate, chopped
¼ cup	strong brewed coffee or water
½ cup	milk
⅓ cup	cocoa powder
⅓ cup	unsalted butter, softened
¾ cup	granulated sugar
2	eggs
1 tsp	vanilla
1 cup	all-purpose flour
½ tsp	each baking soda and baking powder
⅛ tsp	salt

DOUBLE-CHOCOLATE ICING:

½ cup	unsalted butter, softened
1¾ cups	icing sugar
pinch	salt
55 g	milk chocolate, melted and cooled
30 g	unsweetened chocolate, melted and cooled
1 tsp	milk (approx)

How to make it

In heatproof bowl over saucepan of hot (not boiling) water, melt chocolate with coffee, whisking until smooth. Whisk milk with cocoa until smooth; stir into chocolate mixture.

In large bowl, beat butter with sugar until light, about 2 minutes. Beat in eggs, 1 at a time; beat in vanilla. Whisk together flour, baking soda, baking powder and salt; stir into butter mixture alternately with chocolate mixture, making 3 additions of flour mixture and 2 of chocolate mixture, stirring until no streaks remain.

Divide among 12 paper-lined muffin cups. Bake in 350°F (180°C) oven until cake tester inserted in centre of several comes out clean, about 18 minutes.

Let cool in pan on rack for 5 minutes. Transfer to rack; let cool completely.

DOUBLE-CHOCOLATE ICING: In bowl, beat together butter, icing sugar and salt until fluffy, about 4 minutes. Beat in milk chocolate and unsweetened chocolate; beat in milk until smooth, adding up to 1 tsp more if necessary. Spread over cupcakes.

NUTRITIONAL INFORMATION, PER CUPCAKE: about 353 cal, 4 g pro, 19 g total fat (11 g sat. fat), 46 g carb, 2 g fibre, 67 mg chol, 111 mg sodium, 142 mg potassium. % RDI: 4% calcium, 11% iron, 13% vit A, 13% folate.

Banana and Chocolate Malt Cake Cones

HANDS-ON TIME	TOTAL TIME	MAKES
30 MINUTES	1¼ HOURS	18 CONES

What you need

⅔ cup	butter, softened
1 cup	packed brown sugar
2	eggs
1 cup	mashed bananas
1 tsp	vanilla
1⅔ cups	all-purpose flour
¾ tsp	baking powder
½ tsp	baking soda
¼ tsp	each salt and cinnamon
⅓ cup	buttermilk
18	flat-bottom ice cream cups

CHOCOLATE MALT ICING:

¾ cup	chocolate malt drink mix (such as Ovaltine)
2 tbsp	cocoa powder, sifted
¼ cup	icing sugar
½ cup	unsalted butter, softened
150 g	milk chocolate, melted and cooled
2 tsp	coloured sprinkles

How to make it

In large bowl, beat butter with brown sugar until fluffy; beat in eggs, 1 at a time. Beat in bananas and vanilla. Whisk together flour, baking powder, baking soda, salt and cinnamon; stir into butter mixture alternately with buttermilk, making 2 additions of flour mixture and 1 of buttermilk. Scoop into ice cream cups. Set in mini muffin cups.

Bake in 350°F (180°C) oven until cake tester inserted in centre of several cakes comes out clean, about 24 minutes. Let cool on rack.

CHOCOLATE MALT ICING: Meanwhile, in bowl, whisk malt drink mix with cocoa powder; stir in ¼ cup boiling water until smooth. Let cool. Whisk in icing sugar.

In separate bowl, beat butter until creamy; beat in icing sugar mixture. Beat in chocolate until smooth and soft peaks form when beaters are lifted, about 2 minutes.

Spoon icing into piping bag fitted with plain tip; pipe icing onto cones. Garnish with coloured sprinkles. *(Make-ahead: Store in airtight container for up to 24 hours.)*

NUTRITIONAL INFORMATION, PER CONE: about 337 cal, 4 g pro, 16 g total fat (10 g sat. fat), 46 g carb, 2 g fibre, 55 mg chol, 197 mg sodium, 224 mg potassium. % RDI: 5% calcium, 12% iron, 12% vit A, 2% vit C, 21% folate.

Chocolate Caramel Turtle Torte

HANDS-ON TIME	•	TOTAL TIME	•	MAKES
55 MINUTES		2¼ HOURS		12 TO 16 SERVINGS

What you need

115 g	unsweetened chocolate, coarsely chopped
2¼ cups	all-purpose flour
2¼ cups	packed brown sugar
1 tsp	baking soda
½ tsp	baking powder
¼ tsp	salt
1 cup	sour cream
½ cup	butter, softened
3	eggs
1 tsp	vanilla
2 cups	pecan pieces

CARAMEL:

1½ cups	granulated sugar
⅔ cup	whipping cream (35%)
¼ cup	butter

TOPPINGS:

2½ cups	whipping cream (35%)
¾ cup	chocolate shards (see tip, opposite)
⅓ cup	pecan halves, toasted

How to make it

Grease sides of three 9-inch (1.5 L) round cake pans; line bottoms with parchment paper. Set aside.

In heatproof bowl over saucepan of hot (not boiling) water, melt chocolate; let cool slightly. In bowl, whisk together flour, sugar, baking soda, baking powder and salt. Beat in sour cream and butter to make thick batter. Beat in eggs, 1 at a time, beating well after each; beat in chocolate and vanilla. Beat for 2 minutes, scraping down side of bowl occasionally. Gradually stir in 1 cup water.

Divide evenly among prepared pans; sprinkle pecans over tops. Bake in 350°F (180°C) oven until cake tester inserted in centre comes out clean, 30 to 35 minutes. Let cool in pans on racks for 15 minutes. Turn out onto racks; peel off paper. Let cool completely. (Make-ahead: Wrap in plastic wrap and store for up to 1 day.)

CARAMEL: In heavy saucepan, stir sugar with ⅓ cup water over medium heat until dissolved, brushing down side of pan with pastry brush dipped in cold water. Bring to boil; boil hard, without stirring but brushing down side of pan, until dark amber, about 10 minutes. Standing back and averting face, add cream; whisk until smooth. Whisk in butter until smooth. Let cool. (Make-ahead: Refrigerate in airtight container for up to 3 days. Reheat slightly.)

TOPPINGS: Whip cream. Place 1 cake layer, pecan side up, on cake plate. Drizzle with 2 tbsp of the caramel. Spread 1 cup of the whipped cream over top. Drizzle with 2 tbsp of the caramel, being careful not to let any drip down side. Repeat layers once.

Top with remaining cake layer. Spread remaining cream over top and side, smoothing surface. Drizzle 2 tbsp of the caramel over top. Garnish with chocolate shards and pecans. Serve with remaining caramel.

NUTRITIONAL INFORMATION, PER EACH OF 16 SERVINGS: about 685 cal, 7 g pro, 45 g total fat (21 g sat. fat), 71 g carb, 3 g fibre, 124 mg chol, 251 mg sodium. % RDI: 9% calcium, 18% iron, 27% vit A, 2% vit C, 15% folate.

Chocolate Torte With Pecans

HANDS-ON TIME	TOTAL TIME	MAKES
15 MINUTES	1½ HOURS	12 TO 14 SERVINGS

What you need

170 g	bittersweet chocolate, chopped
55 g	milk chocolate, chopped
⅔ cup	whipping cream (35%)
¼ cup	unsalted butter
3	eggs
⅓ cup	packed brown sugar
3 tbsp	all-purpose flour
1 tbsp	bourbon or coffee liqueur
1 cup	coarsely chopped pecans

How to make it

In heatproof bowl over saucepan of hot (not boiling) water, melt together bittersweet chocolate, milk chocolate, cream and butter, stirring occasionally until smooth.

In large bowl, whisk together eggs, brown sugar, flour and bourbon; stir in chocolate mixture just until combined. Fold in pecans.

Scrape into greased 8-inch (2 L) springform pan. Bake in 275°F (140°C) oven until centre is firm to the touch, about 1 hour.

Let cool in pan on rack for 15 minutes. Turn out onto serving plate; let cool. (*Make-ahead: Cover and refrigerate for up to 2 days.*)

TIP FROM THE TEST KITCHEN

To make decorative chocolate shards, in heatproof bowl over a saucepan of hot (not boiling) water, melt 115 g semisweet chocolate, chopped. Spread on a baking sheet; refrigerate until firm, about 15 minutes. Place the baking sheet on a damp towel and let it stand for 3 minutes. Bracing the pan against your body, slowly scrape a metal spatula through the chocolate toward your body to make shards. Refrigerate for 3 to 4 minutes if the chocolate gets too soft to scrape.

NUTRITIONAL INFORMATION, PER EACH OF 14 SERVINGS: about 252 cal, 4 g pro, 29 g total fat (9 g sat. fat), 17 g carb, 2 g fibre, 64 mg chol, 23 mg sodium. % RDI: 4% calcium, 7% iron, 8% vit A, 5% folate.

THANK YOU!

The first people I would like to thank for their hard work on and dedication to this best-of edition are our Food director, Annabelle Waugh, and her team in the Canadian Living Test Kitchen. Chocolate is a passionate indulgence for every one of our food specialists—Irene Fong, Amanda Barnier, Jennifer Bartoli and Gilean Watts. I'm so grateful for their imagination and tireless pursuit of the very best iteration of each of our Tested-Till-Perfect recipes.

Next, thank you to our brilliant art director, Colin Elliott, who reinvented the look of these recipes, giving them a modern, easy-to-follow feel. Working with him is always a treat, but especially so when the subject of the book is this delicious.

Thanks go next to the many talented photographers and stylists who captured the essential beauty of the chocolate recipes in this book. For a complete list of the people who created these images, see right.

Another big thank-you goes to our teams at Juniper Publishing and Simon & Schuster Canada for helping us breathe new life into this book. Their insight and collaborative approach to publishing make our job a pleasure.

Finally, sincerest thanks to Canadian Living's group publisher, Sandra E. Martin, and content director, multiplatform editions, special issues and books, Jessica Ross, for their passion for this and many other projects. Their support means the world to us.

[signature]

TINA ANSON MINE
PROJECT EDITOR

RECIPES
All recipes Tested Till Perfect by the Canadian Living Test Kitchen

PHOTOGRAPHY
Ryan Brook: back cover (left, bottom); p. 144.

Jeff Coulson: back cover (left, second from top); p. 14, 17, 30, 39, 93, 127, 128 and 132.

Yvonne Duivenvoorden: front cover; p. 18, 23, 24, 33, 34, 56, 59, 68, 86, 98, 103, 109, 110, 118, 121, 122, 138 and 147.

Joe Kim: back cover (centre); p. 104 and 148.

Edward Pond: back cover (left, top); p. 11, 40, 64, 114 and 141.

Jodi Pudge: p. 43.

Ryan Szulc: back cover (left, third from top; far right); p. 6, 8, 9, 46, 49, 50, 55, 67, 71, 72, 79, 80, 85, 94 and 97.

FOOD STYLING
Julie Aldis: p. 23.

Donna Bartolini: p. 33.

Ashley Denton: p. 114 and 148.

Carol Dudar: p. 118 and 121.

David Grenier: back cover (left, bottom); p. 144.

Adele Hagan: p. 43 and 127.

Lucie Richard: front cover; p. 34, 56, 59, 110, 122 and 147.

Claire Stancer: p. 98 and 109.

Claire Stubbs: back cover (left, top; centre; far right); p. 6, 8, 9, 11, 17, 18, 24, 40, 46, 49, 50, 55, 64, 68, 79, 86, 103, 104, 138 and 141.

Melanie Stuparyk: back cover (left, second from top); p. 14, 30, 39, 93 and 132.

Nicole Young: back cover (left, third from top); p. 67, 71, 72, 80, 85, 94 and 97.

PROP STYLING
Laura Branson: back cover (left, second from top); p. 30, 39, 43, 127 and 132.

Catherine Doherty: back cover (left, top and bottom; far right); p. 6, 8, 9, 11, 14, 17, 18, 46, 49, 50, 55, 64, 71, 72, 79, 80, 85, 93, 97, 114, 141, 144 and 148.

Marc-Philippe Gagné: p. 24 and 59.

Mandy Gyulay: p. 56.

Madeleine Johari: back cover (left, third from top; centre); p. 67, 94 and 104.

Oksana Slavutych: p. 23, 33, 34, 68, 98, 103, 109, 110, 118, 121, 122 and 138.

Genevieve Wiseman: front cover; p. 40, 86 and 147.

INDEX

Index

Index

Index

About Our Nutrition Information

To meet nutrient needs each day, moderately active women aged 25 to 49 need about 1,900 calories, 51 g protein, 261 g carbohydrate, 25 to 35 g fibre and not more than 63 g total fat (21 g saturated fat). Men and teenagers usually need more. Canadian sodium intake of approximately 3,500 mg daily should be reduced, whereas the intake of potassium from food sources should be increased to 4,700 mg per day. The percentage of recommended daily intake (% RDI) is based on the values used for Canadian food labels for calcium, iron, vitamins A and C, and folate.

Figures are rounded off. They are based on the first ingredient listed when there is a choice and do not include optional ingredients or those with no specified amounts.

ABBREVIATIONS

cal = calories
pro = protein
carb = carbohydrate
sat. fat = saturated fat
chol = cholesterol

Canadian Living

Complete your collection of Tested-Till-Perfect recipes!

Canadian Living: The Ultimate Cookbook

150 Essential Beef, Pork & Lamb Recipes
150 Essential Salads
150 Essential Whole Grain Recipes

New Slow Cooker Favourites

400-Calorie Dinners
Dinner in 30 Minutes or Less
Make It Chocolate!
Pasta & Noodles
Sweet & Simple

The Affordable Feasts Collection
The Appetizer Collection
The Barbecue Collection
The International Collection
The One Dish Collection
The Slow Cooker Collection
The Vegetarian Collection

The Complete Chicken Book
The Complete Chocolate Book
The Complete Preserving Book

Available wherever books are sold or online at
canadianliving.com/books